Call to Action for Science Education

BUILDING OPPORTUNITY FOR THE FUTURE

Committee on the Call to Action for Science Education

Board on Science Education

Division of Behavioral and Social Sciences and Education

Margaret Honey, Heidi Schweingruber, Kerry Brenner, and Phil Gonring, Editors

A Consensus Study Report of

The National Academies of
SCIENCES · ENGINEERING · MEDICINE

The National Academies Press
Washington, D.C.

www.nap.edu

COMMITTEE ON CALL TO ACTION FOR SCIENCE EDUCATION

Margaret A. Honey (*Chair*), President and CEO, New York Hall of Science, NY

Rush D. Holt, CEO Emeritus, American Association for the Advancement of Science, NY

Nancy Hopkins-Evans, Senior Director of State Partnerships, Instruction Partners, PA

Tiffany Neill, Deputy Superintendent for Curriculum and Instruction, Oklahoma State Department of Education

Stephen L. Pruitt, President, Southern Regional Education Board, GA

Francisco Rodriguez, Chancellor, LA Community College District, CA

Susan R. Singer, Vice President for Academic Affairs and Provost, Rollins College, FL

Felicia C. Smith, Senior Director of Global Delivery, National Geographic Society, KY

William F. Tate IV, President, Louisiana State University

Claudio Vargas, Educational Consultant, Sci-Lingual Education, CA

Kerry Brenner, *Study Director*

Elizabeth Sumerlin, *Senior Project Assistant*

Heidi Schweingruber, *Board Director*

Dedication

We dedicate this report to the memory of Vartan Gregorian, president of the Carnegie Corporation of New York, who died on April 15, 2021. This project was one of the last funded by Dr. Gregorian, and we offer this report in honor of his decades of work in science education. This project would not have become a reality without his leadership. He leaves a lasting legacy that will impact generations to come.

CALL TO ACTION FOR SCIENCE EDUCATION

Scientific thinking and understanding are essential for all people navigating the world, not just for scientists and other science, technology, engineering, and mathematics (STEM) professionals.

Contents

Summary   1

Introduction   5

Why Better, More Equitable Science Education Should Be a National Priority   8

A Vision for Better, More Equitable Science Education   14

How Far Are We from This Vision for All Students?   21

How Do We Get There?   30

Recommendations   40

How Can We Learn from These Efforts?   44

In Conclusion   45

References   46

For Further Reading   52

Committee Member Biosketches   59

Acknowledgments   65

Summary

> *Science education is not the national priority it needs to be.*

Science is an essential tool for solving the greatest problems of our time and understanding the world around us. Scientific thinking and understanding are essential for **all people** navigating the world, not just for scientists and other science, technology, engineering, and mathematics (STEM) professionals. They enable people to address complex challenges in local communities and at a global scale, more readily access economic opportunity and, rein in life-threatening problems such as those wrought by a global pandemic. In this way, knowledge of science and the practice of scientific thinking are essential components of a fully functioning democracy. Science is also crucial for the future STEM workforce and the pursuit of living wage jobs. Yet, science education is not the national priority it needs to be, and states and local communities are not yet delivering high-quality, rigorous learning experiences in equal measure to all students from elementary school through higher education.

This report, authored by a committee convened by the National Academies of Sciences, Engineering, and Medicine, lays out a vision for equitable access to quality science learning experiences across K-16 education that will enable all people to develop the scientific literacy they need for personal and professional success. To achieve this vision, investing in improved science learning for all must be a national priority embraced by federal and state policy makers and local communities.

The work of the committee was conducted during the COVID-19 pandemic at a time when our nation is confronting systemic racial and economic inequities that we must end. This context influenced the content of the committee's deliberations, the vision for a **better, more equitable science education** we mapped, and the recommendations we put forth. This report presents our vision, with the aspiration that stakeholders in communities across the country will work together to ensure that, nationwide, students of all races, ethnicities, and financial circumstances have the opportunity to shape the future.

Our vision for K-16 science education is that every student experiences the joy and wonder of science, learns how science can be used to solve local and global problems, sees the pathways they can take into science-related careers, and feels welcomed and valued in science classrooms. This vision is grounded in decades of research on effective teaching and learning. We recognize that many students, particularly students who live in poverty, Black, Latino/a, and Indigenous students, and students living in rural areas, have lacked access to high-quality science education across K-16 and have been shut out of many opportunities in STEM. Addressing the deep and enduring disparities in K-16 science education is paramount.

In this report, we articulate our vision for high-quality science education, describe the gaps in opportunity that currently exist for many students, and outline key priorities that need to be addressed in order to advance **better, more equitable science education** across K-16. These priorities include (1) providing time, materials, and resources for science instruction; (2) developing and supporting a strong, diverse science teaching workforce; (3) designing supportive pathways for students in science; (4) employing well-designed assessments and accountability systems for science; and (5) using evidence to document progress and inform ongoing improvement efforts.

The committee embraces the idea that policy can spur innovation and move an ambitious agenda forward. We recognize that federal, state, and local actors have different roles to play in our education system, and that many of the actions that are needed to realize the promise of science education must be taken at local and regional levels. However, federal and state policy makers and national stakeholders in STEM education can play key roles in supporting the work of local and regional communities as they work to expand opportunities in science education. With this in mind, the committee recommends:

ACTION AREA 1: ELEVATE THE STATUS OF SCIENCE EDUCATION

RECOMMENDATION 1: The White House, with leadership from the Office of Science and Technology Policy (OSTP), should act to raise the profile of science education and elevate the importance of access to high-quality science learning opportunities for all students across K-16. Specifically, OSTP should encourage national stakeholders, including federal agencies, along with those in the education, business, nonprofit, scientific, and philanthropic sectors, to focus resources and leverage their assets to increase the quality of and accessibility to K-16 science education.

RECOMMENDATION 2: Congress should include science as an indicator of academic achievement when it next reauthorizes the Elementary and Secondary Education Act. Accountability for science should focus on students gaining conceptual understanding of science and should not be based on single tests. It should involve a system of assessments and indicators that together provide results that complement each other and provide information about the progress of schools, districts, and states.

RECOMMENDATION 3: State Departments of Education should act now to include science in their accountability systems for K-12 education. A state accountability system for science needs to include assessments that support classroom instruction, assessments that monitor science learning more broadly (at the school, district, and state levels), and indicators that track the availability of high-quality science learning opportunities.

RECOMMENDATION 4: National stakeholders in science, technology, engineering, and mathematics (STEM) education should undertake coordinated advocacy to improve science education K-16 with particular attention to addressing disparities in opportunity. These stakeholders (including professional organizations, advocacy groups, scientists, and business and industry) will need to balance advocacy for STEM broadly with attention to the importance of high-quality learning experiences in science as well as in each of the other STEM disciplines.

ACTION AREA 2: ESTABLISH LOCAL AND REGIONAL ALLIANCES FOR STEM OPPORTUNITY

RECOMMENDATION 5: Leaders of local and regional K-12 systems and postsecondary institutions should work together to form Alliances for STEM Opportunity that involve key stakeholders in science, technology, engineering, and mathematics (STEM) education, such as informal education organizations, nonprofit, afterschool and summer programs, business and industry, and the philanthropic sector. Each alliance should develop an evidence-based vision and plan for improving STEM education that includes specific attention to high-quality science learning opportunities and addresses disparities in opportunity. Plans should include, at minimum, strategies for:

(1) providing access to high-quality science learning experiences across K-16 and addressing existing disparities in access;
(2) providing high-quality instructional materials and other resources to support these experiences;
(3) building a high-quality, diverse workforce for teaching science to include provisions for professional development and ongoing support;
(4) creating pathways for learners in science across grades 6 through 16 with supports for learners who want to pursue STEM careers.

RECOMMENDATION 6: The federal government, philanthropic organizations, and business and industry should provide funding to support the work of local and regional Alliances for STEM Opportunity as they work to improve science education. Funding should be targeted first to communities where a significant number of students live in poverty. Funds should support coordination and management of the alliances, programmatic efforts, and research and evaluation.

ACTION AREA 3: DOCUMENT PROGRESS TOWARD BETTER, MORE EQUITABLE SCIENCE EDUCATION

RECOMMENDATION 7: States should develop and implement data-driven, state-level plans for providing equitable K-16 science, technology, engineering, and mathematics (STEM) education with specific attention to science. These plans should include "STEM Opportunity Maps" that document and track where opportunities are available, where there are disparities in opportunity, and how much progress is being made toward eliminating disparities and achieving the goals of the state STEM education plan. The STEM Opportunity Maps should incorporate documentation from local and regional Alliances for STEM Opportunity.

RECOMMENDATION 8: The federal government should develop an annual "STEM Opportunity in the States" report card that documents the status of K-16 science, technology, engineering, and mathematics (STEM) education across each of the states and territories and tracks equity of opportunity for students in science and in the other STEM disciplines.

Introduction

Over the past 15 months, Americans have had delivered to them a powerful message about why science is essential to the well-being of the United States. The rapid development of COVID-19 vaccines was a 21st century moonshot. We have seen firsthand why science is a powerful public good that we must preserve and prioritize. It is a foundational part of our national infrastructure, essential to our physical health, to the nurturing of an informed citizenry that makes fact-based decisions in everyday life, and to an economy that is becoming increasingly dependent on science, technology, engineering, and mathematics (STEM) fields. Science is remarkable. Yet, as this call to action will demonstrate, science education is not the national priority it needs to be, and states and local communities are not yet delivering high-quality, rigorous learning experiences in equal measure to all students from elementary school through higher education.

> *Over the past 15 months, Americans have had delivered to them a powerful message about why science is essential to the well-being of the United States.*

This report was prepared at the request of the Carnegie Corporation of New York by a consensus committee appointed via the National Academies of Sciences, Engineering, and Medicine. The committee was tasked with developing a national call to action to advance science education programs and instruction across elementary, secondary and postsecondary education in ways that will prepare students to face the global challenges of the future both as engaged participants in society and as future STEM professionals (*see Box 1 for the charge*).

To address their charge, the committee reviewed a large volume of previous National Academies' reports related to science education and analyzed the evidence in those reports most pertinent to policy. We invited a dozen experts on research and practice in K-12 and postsecondary education to speak with them and collected input from more than 700 public comments, as well as contributions assembled by the National Science

BOX 1: STATEMENT OF TASK

The National Academies of Sciences, Engineering, and Medicine will appoint an ad hoc committee to author a national call to action to advance science education programs and instruction in K-12 and postsecondary institutions in ways that will prepare students to face the global challenges of the future both as engaged participants in society and as future STEM professionals. The call will draw on the National Academies' existing body of work in K-12 and undergraduate STEM education.

Specially, the call will

- Provide an argument for the importance of science education across K-16
- Identify the major challenges for implementing coherent science education K-16
- Discuss how science relates to the other STEM disciplines in K-16
- Describe the approaches to science education program and instructional practices that have shown to be most effective
- Provide recommendations for policy makers at the state and federal level to advance and strengthen science education K-16 programs and instructional practices
- Identify areas where more information is needed about how best to advance science education K-16

Teaching Association from more than 1,000 of their members. The committee synthesized the evidence and input to prepare this call to action for federal, state, and local policy makers.

The committee calls on the policy-making community at state and federal levels to acknowledge the importance of science, make science education a core national priority, and empower and give local communities the resources they must have to deliver a **better, more equitable science education** and track progress. We call for a new locally grounded approach, bolstered by state and national support, in which community members and leaders work together to ensure widespread, consistent, coherent opportunities for high-quality science learning are available to all students across K-16 and that people of all backgrounds are welcomed in science learning environments, in STEM careers, and as contributors and decision makers in their own communities.

CALL TO ACTION FOR SCIENCE EDUCATION

In the next section of our call to action, we explain why state and federal policy makers should elevate science to a national priority, and include arguments related to our nation's economic growth, the health of our democracy, and the ongoing struggle to bring greater racial and gender equity[1] to the United States. We then articulate a vision for what **better, more equitable science education** looks like, the benefits it brings, and the obstacles that stand in its way. We conclude by laying out a set of recommendations that if enacted will help the nation make this vision a reality. This report is designed to highlight broad, evidence-based strategies for improving science education and to provide information to support the policy makers we call on to act. It does not provide detailed guidance on changes at the institution or classroom level. Extensive information on strategies for those levels can be found in other publications from the National Academies as described in the section at the end of this report on "For Further Reading."

In summary, the eight recommendations we make call for federal and state policy makers to (1) elevate the status of science education, (2) foster the creation of local and regional alliances to advance **better, more equitable science education** across communities, and (3) institutionalize mechanisms to track progress and determine where there are disparities in access to high-quality science learning experiences so that resources can be directed to where they are needed most.

---

[1] Equity is the distribution of goods and/or services in a manner that provides additional resources to the neediest people. This definition is adopted from the National Academies report *Monitoring Educational Equity* (2019) [1].

CALL TO ACTION FOR SCIENCE EDUCATION

Why Better, More Equitable Science Education Should Be a National Priority

Science is an essential tool for solving the greatest problems of our time and understanding the world around us.

The pandemic has put on display for all to see the profound impact of science. Scientists around the word mobilized with breathtaking speed to isolate the devastating new coronavirus and take vaccines to scale in under a year.

Through science we have reached pinnacles of human achievement: the moon landings of the 1960s, the Hubble Telescope, the exploration of our deepest oceans, better understanding of the human body and human behavior, the development of treatments from gene therapy to robotic body parts to replace amputated limbs, and the discovery of water on Mars.

The accomplishments and discoveries of science are inspirational, especially for children, as they come to understand their world and develop a sense of agency within it. Science education needs to stimulate children's intellect and imagination and motivate them to consider science as they work to solve the pressing problems the world faces today and will confront tomorrow: cancer, future outbreaks of disease, tenacious agricultural challenges, climate change, food insecurity, and disparities in health and wellness between racial groups, to name just a few. America needs a rich and diverse pool of talent to solve the problems of the future. When solutions are designed from many perspectives, they can better address the needs of diverse communities.

Scientific thinking and understanding are essential for all people navigating the world, not just for scientists and other STEM professionals. A big mistake the country has made is believing that science is for scientists only. Science should be taught with all people in mind, not just to fill the pipeline for future scientists and technical workers. The nation's schools teach reading, writing, and mathematics because these are foundational skills for daily life and participation in society. **Science literacy is fundamental as well.**

All people need scientific literacy to be critical consumers in their everyday activities and to make sense of information presented in traditional or social media [2]. Americans need to be able to evaluate evidence and distinguish between what are reliable sources of information, poorly supported claims, and unequivocal falsehoods. Again, the pandemic shows why. The press and government officials have shared new findings related to COVID-19 on an almost daily basis. The regular flow of information about the virus demands constant evaluation of new evidence to inform decisions that impact daily lives: whether to go to the grocery store, cancel a child's birthday party, or send them to school. The past year has demonstrated the need for everyone to understand science at its most basic levels. **Simply put, scientific literacy elevates the quality of decision making in almost every aspect of daily life.**

Science does not replace values, ethics, faith, and aesthetics; rather, it provides people with the means for understanding the world in which they apply all those things. Neglect, misunderstanding, or rejection of science resulted in tragic surges of the pandemic. It is apparent that the country needs millions of trained, creative scientists and support technicians, and it is apparent also that large numbers of world-class scientists are not a substitute for an entire citizenry that understands and embraces science. Science in society and in the schools must be for all, not only for reasons of fairness and equity, but also so that a democratic society can deal with the problems that confront it.

Understanding science and the practice of scientific thinking are essential components of a fully functioning democracy. Many of the nation's and communities' most pressing social and political issues involve science. Civic leaders, community members, and voters need to make informed decisions about policies and investments that often require some consideration of scientific evidence. For example, decisions about how a community can maintain air quality, whether it should consider flood or air pollution mitigation, whether to institute water rationing during a drought, and what to do about the proliferation of plastics all require people to grapple with the underlying science. In fact, responding to any issue, even those that do not appear to pertain to science, requires that people ask the question that science teaches students to ask and answer, "What does the evidence suggest?"

27% people of color in the U.S. population

11% people of color in STEM professions

This question is a tool that civic and state leaders have used frequently during the pandemic when presented with the need to regularly update guidance on when and how to open restaurants and businesses, how many people to allow at sporting events, how to conduct high school athletics, and when and how to reopen schools —and at what grade levels. Science is one of the key disciplines that teaches people how to ground decision making in evidence.

Science is also crucial for the future STEM workforce and the pursuit of living wage jobs. While STEM skills have always been important for many kinds of technical work, these skills are becoming increasingly valuable for an array of jobs held by workers who have not traditionally been thought of as part of the science labor force, such as welders, electricians, and farmers [3]. (*See Box 2 for how science is essential to farming.*) Still, the nation needs a cadre of talented scientists, engineers, and other STEM professionals to advance knowledge, design new technology, and drive a robust economy. The opportunity to be among that cadre should be equitably distributed across all geographies and populations of students, including people of color and women. STEM jobs are much more likely to secure living wages for those employed in them. The U.S. Bureau of Labor Statistics reports that in 2019, the wage of a STEM professional averaged $86,980. For a non-STEM worker, it was $38,160. That's a difference of nearly $50,000 annually [4].

CALL TO ACTION FOR SCIENCE EDUCATION

BOX 2: SCIENCE IS ESSENTIAL TO FARMING

Farmers are some of America's greatest citizen scientists. "American farmers are among the best scientists in the nation," says Ross Steward, who manages the Limited Irrigation Research Farm, a 40-acre experimental farm operated by the U.S. Department of Agriculture's Agriculture Research Service in Northern Colorado. "They're always experimenting with what works best in individual fields, how to rotate crops, what seed variety to use and what tillage, pest management and irrigation practices work best and under what conditions."

Though Steward grew up in suburban Denver, he frequently worked his family farm in western Nebraska, where he fell in love with agriculture. After high school, he earned an associate degree from the Nebraska College of Technical Agriculture (NCTA), a 2-year college in Curtis, Nebraska. There he took scientific coursework in soil science, plant physiology, crop management and other agricultural science courses to develop skills every farmer needs, such as marketing, economics, and welding.

Steward works closely with a team of four scientists, two plant physiologists and two agricultural engineers, who focus on the Limited Irrigation Research Farm's primary mission: crop water research for semi-arid climates. The experimental farm is located on Colorado's front range, part of America's high plains region that covers the Texas Panhandle and parts of New Mexico, Montana, Wyoming, South Dakota, and Oklahoma, in addition to Colorado. Colorado's front range—particularly the Denver metro area—is experiencing explosive population growth, and the experimental lab is working to find ways to ensure that there's enough water to go around in a region that experiences little rainfall and where more frequent droughts are anticipated.

The plant physiologists study how plants handle stress and adapt. "One way to accomplish this is to conduct genotype studies and monitor how different varieties handle water stress. Once you find a genotype that exhibits the results you want, you study the plants to identify what traits they have to better handle stress. That's critical information that can be used in future crop breeding and potentially making genetic modifications," Steward says. "The goal is to find and develop crops that require much less water."

The plant physiologists work side-by-side with the agricultural engineers, who develop and study remote sensing technology—in particular how to "take information from a plant without touching it, using drones, and RBG or thermal imagery," Steward says.

To disseminate knowledge the farm produces, the scientists publish papers and also host field days for farmers, water rights lawyers, and agricultural associations, such as the Colorado Corn Association and the Colorado Wheat Growers Association. "But science can't be a one-way street," Steward says. "Farmers know their land better than anyone else. They need to be invited into the conversation with scientists because farmers are researchers too. They are experts that scientists need to listen to."

SOURCE: Personal communication to Phil Gonring, April 2, 2021.

CALL TO ACTION FOR SCIENCE EDUCATION

Yet, the nation has a poor track record of advancing students of color[2] out of K-12, into postsecondary learning opportunities, and on to STEM professions. Black, Latino/a, and American Indian/Alaska native people make up 27 percent of the U.S. population ages 21 and older but occupy only 11 percent of STEM positions [5]. Women are also underrepresented in many STEM fields. Only 15 percent of engineers and 26 percent of those employed in computer and mathematical science fields are women [5]. In not providing pathways for so many people to enter STEM careers, the country is missing out on their talents and limiting their futures.

Science Must Be Equitable and Inclusive

Science must not remain a club for a few. There is ample evidence that workforce diversity produces better, more innovative results. Diversity in the workplace not only expands the available talent pool, but also increases the range of perspectives and expertise available to solve grand challenges in STEM [6]. Diversity in the workplace, particularly the STEM workforce, also improves work performance and engagement, enhances the quality of research and provision of health care, and supports innovation and growth [7, 8, 9]. Research has also shown that corporations with intentional efforts to recruit and promote people of color and women are more profitable [10]. And scientific research groups that are more heterogeneous, based on gender, produce research that is more likely to be published in high-impact journals [11].

Beyond benefits to the scientific enterprise, expanding the pool of talent is important for ensuring that science takes up questions and problems that are important for a

---

[2]For the purposes of this report, "people of color" is a term we use to signify those who identify as Black, Latino/a, Asian/Pacific Islander, and Indigenous/Native American/Alaska Native. We opt to use the more contemporary term "Latino/a" in place of the term "Hispanic," which commonly appears in datasets we draw from. When quoting directly from datasets, we use their terms. Different researchers, when they are identifying students who are underrepresented, either include or exclude Asian, especially when identifying populations underrepresented in STEM. We have footnoted places where it is important to understand what dataset the research we cite uses.

wide range of communities. Building a diverse scientific workforce can help ensure that science better serves all people.

Science Education and STEM Education

For over a decade, the importance of giving students pathways into STEM professions has guided STEM education in the United States. Efforts have largely been focused on inspiring students to pursue STEM careers. This emphasis can lead to programs that target select groups of students and may overlook the importance of science and mathematics as foundational disciplines for all students.

In fact, science is foundational to technology and engineering and provides the basis for the entire modern technical sector. Science is the questioning, the systematic observations, the measurement and data collection, the experimentation and modeling, and the process for revising knowledge based on new evidence that underlies the STEM disciplines. For students to develop foundational knowledge and competency in science, they will need to have access to high-quality learning experiences focused on science. Activities that integrate across the STEM disciplines can be motivating, but they cannot replace high-quality science instruction for all students to help them understand the practices and principles of the discipline.

A Vision for Better, More Equitable Science Education

Our vision is that every student experiences the joy, beauty and power of science, learns how science can be used to solve local and global problems, sees the pathways they can take into science-related careers, and feels welcomed and valued in science classrooms.

We call on policy makers to embrace a national vision for science education that can guide efforts across the country to create the conditions for elementary and secondary schools, and postsecondary institutions to provide **better, more equitable science education** for all students. Our vision is that every student experiences the joy, beauty, and power of science, learns how science can be used to solve local and global problems, sees the pathways they can take into science-related careers, and feels welcomed and valued in science classrooms. Providing high-quality science learning experiences is the core of this vision. The good news is that research and experience provide a clear picture of what high-quality science education can and should look like.

High-Quality Science Teaching and Learning

To provide high-quality teaching and learning in science, our nation, states, and communities must reframe the way they think about students from kindergarten through college. Students do not learn best by passively soaking up bits of information and then regurgitating it through multiple-choice tests and other simple measures designed to assess factual knowledge [12]. Rather, from the earliest ages, children and youth are actively working to make sense of the world. They are capable of asking questions, gathering data, evaluating evidence, and generating new insights, just as professional scientists do [13].

Currently, however, far too many students at all levels are learning science by reading about it in a textbook, sitting back and passively listening to lectures, and memorizing disconnected facts [14, 15, 16, 17]. These approaches leave many students bored and asking a question that is far too often uttered in American schools: "What does science have to do with my life?" Worse, too many students perceive science as inaccessible, as a discipline consigned to an elite few who are willing to persist in a system that uses antiquated instructional practices. Worse still, lacking role models, students of color may not consider science as a potential career. The end result is that our nation ends up retaining a few and weeding out many—a practice that results in substantial inequities and an American citizenry of science "haves" and science "have-nots" [18].

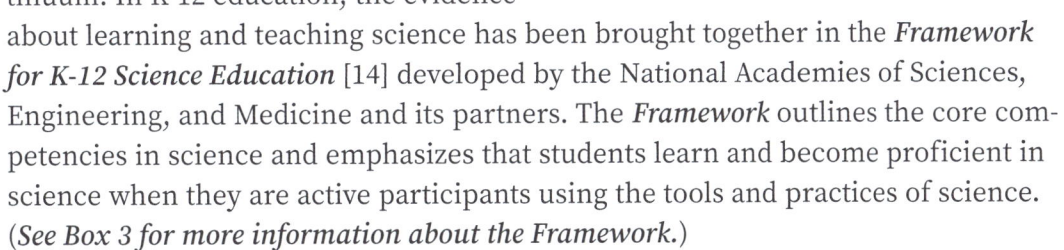

Our vision for science classrooms is informed by what is known about how students learn, regardless of where they are on the education continuum. In K-12 education, the evidence about learning and teaching science has been brought together in the *Framework for K-12 Science Education* [14] developed by the National Academies of Sciences, Engineering, and Medicine and its partners. The *Framework* outlines the core competencies in science and emphasizes that students learn and become proficient in science when they are active participants using the tools and practices of science. (*See Box 3 for more information about the Framework.*)

If a person wants to learn to play the trumpet, they need to blow air into it, figure out how to position their lips on the mouthpiece, and what valves to press to produce the right sounds. They need to experiment and discover, not read about trumpet playing in a book. The same applies to learning science. Reading about science in a book, listening to someone talk about it, or memorizing key terms will not get the job done.

BOX 3: TRANSFORMING K-12 SCIENCE EDUCATION

The *Framework for K-12 Science Education: Practices, Crosscutting Concepts and Core Ideas* [15] catalyzed an ongoing transformation of elementary and secondary science education across the United States. The *Framework* provides guidance for improving science education that builds on previous national standards for science education and reflects research-based advances in learning and teaching science.

As of April 2020, 44 states and the District of Columbia had developed and adopted science standards that are informed by or directly based on the *Framework*. This represents approximately 70 percent of K-12 public school students.

The vision for science education outlined in the *Framework* differs in important ways from how science has traditionally been taught. It emphasizes engaging students in using the tools and practices of science and engineering and providing them with opportunities to explore phenomena and problems that are relevant to them and to their communities.

For example, elementary students in classrooms that reflect the vision of the *Framework* might explore what happens to the garbage from their school cafeteria. This may begin with students investigating their questions about why garbage smells so bad. Over the course of a unit, they will have opportunities to explore bigger issues such as what happens to the large amounts of garbage schools, homes, and communities make each day. Through their investigations and discussions, students learn to explain how microbes break down food, what a gas is, and why plastics do not decompose in the same way as organic material. They will even have the tools to think about how communities can better manage the garbage they produce (see http://www.nyusail.org/curriculum for more details).

Similarly, middle school students may pursue the question of why a dropped cell phone sometimes results in a shattered screen and sometimes does not. Students' questions about the factors that result in a shattered cell phone screen lead them to investigate what is really happening to any object during a collision. They conduct experiments and record what happens when different kinds of objects collide. They create diagrams, mathematical models, and system models to explain the effects of relative forces, mass, speed, and energy in collisions. They then use what they have learned about collisions to engineer something that will protect a fragile object from damage in a collision. They investigate which materials to use, gather design input from stakeholders to refine the criteria and constraints, develop micro and macro models of how their solution is working, and optimize their solution based on data from investigations (see http://www.openscied.org/instructional-materials/8-1-contact-forces/ for more details).

Science educators, professional organizations, non-profits, and philanthropic organizations have been devoting countless hours and resources to making the vision of the *Framework* a reality. Their efforts are providing a growing compendium of resources for curriculum, professional development, and assessment many of which are freely available online. There are also many local, regional, and national networks of science educators who are supporting each other in vibrant communities of practice as they work to implement high-quality science learning and teaching in their classrooms. Our call to action can build on and accelerate these efforts.

In the same way, students across elementary, secondary, and postsecondary education need opportunities to do the things that scientists do: pose questions, carry out investigations, analyze data, draw evidence-based conclusions, and communicate results in various ways. They need to engage with scientific phenomena and, as scientists do, debate with peers to develop the conceptual understanding of science that leads to factual understanding as well [13, 14, 15]. (*See Box 4 for more information about high-quality postsecondary science.*)

Science should also be meaningful and relevant to students so that they no longer ask, "What does this have to do with my life?" In the classrooms we envision, students will be able to make connections between the experiences they have in their homes and communities and the content they are learning in science [14]. When educators limit science teaching to a set of facts to be memorized, they subvert students' natural inclination to grapple with problems that are real to them. Meaningful science experiences that provide opportunities for students to explore questions they are passionate about foster the development of critical thinking and scientific skills, reinforce that science is relevant to students' daily lives, and inspire them to consider science-related fields as career paths.

A Well-Prepared, Diverse Science Teaching Workforce

Teachers of science at all levels are the key to fulfilling a vision for high-quality, engaging, active, student-centered learning. To implement a vision of **better, more equitable science education,** teachers of science need to be fluent in the subject matter they teach and fluent in the pedagogy of effective science instruction, including how to promote the success of culturally and linguistically diverse students in the context of science [19]. Effective teachers of science understand that their job is not merely to impart knowledge but rather provide opportunities for students to build their knowledge through problem solving and experimentation. In their classrooms, students learn by doing. Teachers play a key role as facilitators of small teams of student scientists working to conduct investigations, gather evidence, and discuss and debate with teammates what conclusions they can draw from the evidence. They know how to set up open-ended investigations through which students may arrive at and debate different conclusions that are always based on logical reasoning, evidence, and analysis. They recognize that communication in all forms is an essential part of science, and that in addition to teaching science, they are building critical communication skills. Their teaching is grounded in the belief that every student can succeed in the science classroom and it is their job to support those who are struggling.

BOX 4: HIGH-QUALITY POSTSECONDARY SCIENCE

Faculty, instructors, education researchers, and directors of Centers for Teaching and Learning have been devoting countless hours and resources to transforming undergraduate STEM education [83, 84, 85]. They are working to help faculty and others who teach postsecondary students adopt a more inclusive evidenced based approach to their teaching. They are working locally on campuses and nationally through diverse networks focused on a particular discipline (such as physics, biology or geosciences) or approach (such as course based undergraduate research or higher quality instructional resources) that can make instruction engaging to a wide variety of learners [86, 87, 88, 89, 90, 91]. Our call to action can leverage and accelerate these efforts. It can lead to more students engaged in relevant rewarding science learning experiences in which they lead discussions, analyze case studies, learn as a team, and problem solve in the process of learning scientific principles and practices.

For example, Elizabeth Nagy-Shadman of Pasadena City College uses activities, materials, and assessments developed by InTeGrate for a nonmajors course in Physical Geology [92]. Her community college students study efforts to improve crop yields to support growing populations in areas where current agricultural practices are not sustainable. The unit culminates in a summative assessment that asks students to create a fact sheet that describes local soil properties required for plant fertility, the relationship between potential climate changes and soil erosion rates, and ultimately to make recommendations for specific agriculture practices that will make soil sustainable, while taking into account the needs of farmers. Throughout the module, students engage in active learning, including think/pair/share activities during which two students work together to produce brief answers to prompts related to reading assignments or other content; small-group work to record observations and think critically about soil samples in response to well-crafted questions; and whole-group discussion designed to foster debate and consensus-building around key issues related to soil, erosion, and agriculture.

Effective teaching practice does not come about by accident. It is the result of providing teachers with opportunities to learn throughout their teaching careers [16, 19]. This includes knowledge of science, an initial foundation in effective student-centered pedagogy in science, and culturally and linguistically responsive practice, even for teachers of science in higher education. To continue to build on this initial foundation, all teachers of science across K-16 need ample opportunities to engage in ongoing professional learning focused specifically on science pedagogy, and to participate in professional communities in which members observe each other's practice and provide feedback, solve problems together, and refine classroom activities and units.

We envision a K-16 education system that prioritizes and values the quality of science teaching and recognizes teachers of science at all levels as professionals. In this vision, elementary, secondary, and postsecondary teachers of science feel supported by their institutional leaders who advocate for their ongoing learning and recognize its importance. This is especially important in postsecondary education where professional demands and reward structures may not emphasize teaching. Teachers from groups that are underrepresented among science teachers—Black, Latino/a, and Indigenous teachers across K-16 and women in some postsecondary institutions [20, 21, 22, 23] —will feel welcome and valued, with the result that there is a diverse body of science educators who look more like America. This also means that more students have the opportunity to connect with science teachers who look like them.

Supportive Pathways Through Science

Students' opportunities to learn science by doing science need to continue across K-12 and into their postsecondary experiences. As they move into high school and college, they will need expanded opportunities to learn science through internships, apprenticeships, and foundational research experiences [24].

In our vision, students who are interested in pursuing science or STEM-related careers have clear pathways to follow and encounter few barriers transitioning between different institutions [16]. Higher education makes it a priority to broaden opportunity for populations of students underrepresented in STEM professions and produces science and engineering graduates of all races and ethnicities in at least proportion to their percentage share of the American population. (*See Box 5 for an example of the pathways taken by a life-saving scientist.*)

In this vision, all students finishing postsecondary programs or degrees leave understanding even more deeply than they did upon high school graduation how science and scientific thinking are relevant to their careers and lives. Those receiving STEM degrees are specialists in their area of interest, prepared to succeed in the workforce, or pursue post baccalaureate degrees after participating in rigorous, relevant, student-centered coursework and undergraduate research opportunities.

If the nation fulfills this vision and extends the opportunity for a high-quality science education to all, the question, "What does science have to do with my life?" should disappear from the lexicon of students. America will thrive as a nation of science "haves."

BOX 5: A LIFE-SAVING SCIENTIST

Of Kizzmekia Corbett and the Moderna COVID-19 vaccine, Anthony Fauci, head of the National Institute of Allergy and Infectious Disease, says, "The vaccine you are going to be taking was developed by an African American woman, and that is just a fact." Corbett is a 35-year-old immunologist and lead scientist for coronavirus research at the National Institutes of Health.

In collaboration with Moderna, Corbett's lab designed a vaccine for COVID-19 in just 2 days after receiving genomic sequence for the virus from Chinese scientists. A mere 66 days after the genetic code of the virus was identified, including a period during which Corbett designed and led tests of the vaccine on animals, the National Institutes of Health and Moderna began clinical trials on humans.

The rapid development of the vaccine was in large part due to Corbett's prior research on immune responses to coronaviruses. The 6-year effort and the knowledge it engendered allowed her lab to develop the vaccine at a record rate. To put this achievement in perspective, 4 years was the previous record for vaccine development, from the isolation of the Mumps virus in the 1960s to approval [93].

Corbett grew up in rural North Carolina and went to an elementary school in an area surrounded by soybean and tobacco farms. Her fourth-grade teacher recognized her talent and insisted to her mother that she was special and should attend advanced reading and math classes: "She had so much knowledge. She knew something about everything." She became a high school math whiz and while a high school sophomore she joined Project SEED, a program for low-income students and students of color. As a member of the program, she did research at the University of North Carolina at Chapel Hill.

Corbett went on to attend the University of Maryland—Baltimore County as an undergraduate and Meyerhoff Scholar. The Meyerhoff Scholars Program aims to increase diversity in science, technology, and engineering among those who plan to earn doctorates in the field. At the university, Corbett earned a scholarship to do undergraduate research on syncytial virus, an upper respiratory disease that is serious for the elderly and infants. She went on to earn an undergraduate degree in biological sciences with a secondary major in sociology and then a doctorate in microbiology and immunology from the University of North Carolina at Chapel Hill. In addition to leading a team that focuses on coronavirus vaccines and novel therapeutic antibodies, she has also devoted many years to developing a universal influenza vaccine and has studied dengue fever.

Corbett has also been working as an advocate for COVID-19 vaccinations, especially in communities of color. She has been meeting virtually with church groups to discuss the importance of getting vaccinated and to respond to questions and concerns, explaining science in what she says is a digestible way. She says that it is important in churches to "have something scientifically broken down … by someone who also believes in God. It's not about what you're saying, it's about how you relate to the people you're saying it to."

SOURCE: Case developed based on stories in Nature, The Washington Post, CBS News, and UNC Health Talk [93, 94, 95, 96].

How Far Are We from This Vision for All Students?

While there are many strong examples of high-quality science education across the country, science remains an afterthought in too many communities. In the United States, whether rich or poor, Black, Latino/a, Pacific Islander, Native American/Alaska Native, Asian, or White, too few are receiving the rich science instruction and experiences they need. However, within and across districts and within and across states, there exist wide disparities in access to high-quality learning experiences, well-prepared teachers, high-quality curriculum and curriculum-based professional learning, instructional materials, and assessments. Students of color and students experiencing poverty are particularly unlikely to have high-quality science learning experiences across K-16. Here we focus on illuminating the situation today and the opportunity gaps that currently exist.

Within and across districts and within and across states, there exist wide disparities in access to high-quality learning experiences in science.

K-12 Science Education

Only 22 percent of American high school graduates are proficient in science [25]. It is not hard to understand why. The average American elementary classroom devotes less than 20 minutes per day to science, but nearly 90 minutes to English/Language Arts and nearly 1 hour to mathematics [26]. This is likely in part due to the unintended consequence of state school accountability systems built as a result of No Child Left Behind (NCLB) and its successor, the Every Student Succeeds Act. The law mandates

20 minutes per day to science

90 minutes per day to English/Language Arts

60 minutes per day to mathematics

Average time spent per day in elementary classrooms.

testing in reading and mathematics in grades 3-8 and once in high school but requires an assessment in science only once in each grade-band, K-5, 6-8 and 9-12. It does not require science to be built into state accountability systems. There has been a decline in the time spent on elementary science since 2000, the year NCLB was passed [27]. There is wide variation across states in how much time for science is required in elementary school [27]. In states that include science in accountability for fourth grade, fourth-grade teachers report spending more time on science [28].

Less exposure to science in elementary school could be problematic for students who do not have access to science learning opportunities in their homes and communities [13]. For these students, limiting early science learning opportunities in school may leave them unprepared for science courses in middle and high school [29].

In addition to challenges in the time spent on science in elementary, there are challenges in providing high-quality science learning experiences across K-12. While some K-12 students today carry out investigations, analyze data, draw evidence-based conclusions, and communicate results, few students have these kinds of high-quality science learning experiences consistently across their educational journeys. Many students still experience more traditional science classes that are not grounded in the evidence about how people learn [30]. In a nationally representative survey of science teachers, less than one-half reported using the kinds of instructional practices we are calling for at least once a week; only about 25 percent reported that they place heavy emphasis on increasing students' interest in science [26]. **There is also a substantial opportunity gap**; students in high poverty elementary and middle schools are less likely than students in more affluent schools to do "hands-on" work every week [30].

And for many students, instructional materials, supplies, and other critical curriculum resources are insufficient. High-quality **instructional resources** are starting to be more available, but many students are still provided with out-of-date textbooks and have their laboratory or investigation work limited by a lack of material and supplies [31, 26]. The lack of science facilities is also a problem [31]. Elementary and middle school students in schools that enroll high percentages of students living in poverty have less access to space to conduct investigations and are far less likely to have ample supplies to support the investigations they do conduct than their peers in schools where students are more affluent [30]. The pandemic also revealed the sharp disparities in access to technology to support learning including lack of adequate broad band services, which is a particular problem for low-income families and in rural areas [32].

Having an underprepared, nondiverse teaching workforce is also a challenge.
In a recent national survey, the majority of elementary teachers (69%) reported they are not very well prepared to teach science, and scores of secondary teachers say they are not very well prepared to teach many topics related to their disciplines [26]. This is the case even in well-resourced schools. For example, 36 percent of biology teachers in these schools report that they are not very well prepared to teach cell biology, and 39 percent ecology and ecosystems. Sixty-three percent of physics teachers report they do not feel very well prepared to teach properties of waves [26].

not very well prepared to teach cell biology

not very well prepared to teach ecology & ecosystems

not very well prepared to teach properties of waves

Teachers' perceptions of their preparation to teach topics in their discipline.

The problem of teachers' lack of preparation to teach science is more acute in schools that serve higher percentages of students of color and students living in poverty. In these schools, students are more likely to be taught by inexperienced teachers and, in secondary schools, are less likely to be taught by a teacher with a relevant degree or advanced courses in the subject taught [33].

Further, far too many school districts have difficulty recruiting, hiring and retaining licensed STEM teachers [34]. Staffing shortages are more acute in schools that serve higher percentages of students living in poverty and in rural areas. Staffing patterns vary across states and are highly localized partly because teachers tend to work close to where they did their training [20] (*See Box 6 for information about challenges for STEM education in rural areas.*).

The science teaching corps is also not diverse. Eight of 10 public elementary, middle school, and high school science teachers are White [35], denying students of color the role models that drive greater effort in school and foster higher college goals [36]. There are particular difficulties with attracting and retaining teachers of color. Teachers of color are more likely to work in schools that are in high-poverty, urban communities and they are more likely to change schools or leave the profession than White teachers. These higher rates of turnover may be tied to poor working conditions in the schools where teachers of color are more likely to work [37].

Science students in high-poverty secondary schools, rural schools, and schools with high numbers of students of color are less likely to be enrolled in college prep courses. Data from the National Center for Education Statistics show that White students are more likely to earn their highest-level science credit in an Advanced Placement or International Baccalaureate course than Black and Latino/a students. Black and Latino/a students also amass fewer years of high school science credit on average than do White students [38].

Similarly, high-poverty schools are at least 1.5 times as likely as low-poverty schools to lack advanced coursework in mathematics and science [1]. For example, 14 percent of

BOX 6: RURAL STUDENTS AND EQUITY OF OPPORTUNITY IN STEM

"Many of the 9 million students enrolled in rural schools in the United States face barriers to a high-quality STEM education: shortages of mathematics and science teachers, high teacher turnover, and few resources. But with a STEM education becoming so fundamental to success in any industry, finding ways to improve the quality of STEM learning everywhere is of critical importance to educators and policy makers," says Pamela Buffington of the Education Development Center [97]. Denise Harshbarger, who in 2014 was the supervisor for special projects at the North East Florida Education Consortium, a rural-serving organization, adds, "They're having a hard time keeping up, largely due to money as well as [teacher] recruitment and retention. And if you don't have the teachers who are really able to know STEM subjects, then you're not going to be able to catch students up with the curve" [98].

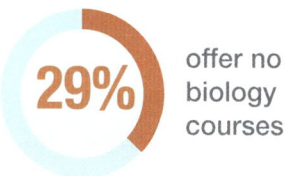 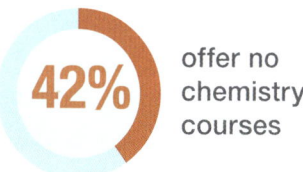 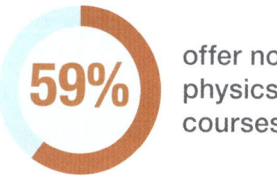

Science course offerings in schools where at least 80% of students are Black, Latino/a, or Indigenous.

schools that enroll the fewest numbers of Black, Latino/a and Indigenous students offer no biology courses, 18 percent offer no chemistry courses and 31 percent offer no physics courses. In contrast, in schools that enroll large percentages of Black, Latino/a and Indigenous students, 29 percent offer no biology courses, 42 percent offer no chemistry courses, and 59 percent offer no physics courses [39]. Similar trends in lack of access to science courses can be seen in schools enrolling significant numbers of students living at or below the poverty line [39]. For schools to offer these courses, they need to be able to hire teachers who have the science background required to teach them.

Disparities exist for rural students as well. In 2015, the percent of rural high school seniors (62%) who had access to at least one Advanced Placement STEM course was substantially lower than seniors in urban (88%) and suburban schools (93%). The percentage of rural students (48%) in that same year who scored a 3 or higher on their STEM Advanced Placement exam was also lower than urban (52%) and suburban (62%) students [40].

These patterns in access and course-taking have implications for whether students are able to smoothly transition to postsecondary education. Some state university systems have course-taking requirements for entry that are more difficult to meet in schools that do not routinely offer all the necessary courses [41].

Taken together these opportunity gaps make clear why there are performance differences in science between White students and their Black, Hispanic, and Native American and Alaska Native peers. The 2015 National Assessment of Educational Progress (NAEP) for Science (administered to fourth, eighth and twelfth graders) revealed performance gaps between White students and students form these racial groups no lower than 26 and as high as 34 points on a 300-point scale. The 2015 NAEP assessment also revealed 33- and 27-point differentials between fourth- and eighth-grade students on free and reduced lunch and those not enrolled in the program [25].

Postsecondary Education

Even students who are qualified to enter postsecondary education do not always continue on after high school graduation. There is evidence that students experiencing poverty are more likely to change their postsecondary plans. The phenomenon known as "summer melt," in which enrolled students do not show up for the fall semester, is much more common for students experiencing poverty, those who attended large city school districts, and those originally planning to attend community college. Rates can be as high as 40 percent for these groups, compared to 10-20 percent for others [42].

There are also regional variations in access to postsecondary institutions that can shape the paths students take after high school. For a variety of reasons—jobs, family, cost, ties to the community—many students choose to pursue postsecondary education close to home. Uneven geographic distribution of colleges and universities means that in some areas of the country students do not have access to a public college option, or to a college that matches their level of academic credentials [43, 44]. This is more likely to be the case in rural or moderately sized communities leaving students in these communities with fewer options [43, 44].

Quality of science instruction is also a problem in postsecondary education. Lecturing is still prominent in undergraduate STEM courses; one study reported it was used on average 75 percent of the time and that students spent an average of 87 percent of their class time listening to instructors [45]. While White students reported the fewest negative effects resulting from poor quality STEM teaching, students of color were more likely to blame themselves for learning problems instead of the poor teaching [46]. While instructors also used some class time for group work, posing questions, and student writing, even flexible classroom layouts and small course sizes did not necessarily lead to an increase in these or other student-centered practices. This suggests that multiple changes, likely including pedagogical training, are needed to raise the quality of teaching [45].

Pathways into and through postsecondary science become complex as students take courses in more than one institution and may step in and out of enrollment [16]. The complex array of pathways that students can take to obtain science degrees is not easily navigated, and students encounter barriers of many types along the path to earning a degree [16]. The environments they encounter when they begin college may not be welcoming, in addition to the low-quality teaching described above. Barriers also result from departmental, institutional, and national policies. Students may find themselves inadequately prepared for the rigor of college coursework or they may face stereotypes from faculty or peers [16]. They also report that it can be challenging to receive academic help or advising [46]. Therefore, these barriers apply to classrooms experiences as well as impacting other aspects of campus life.

The weed-out culture in which a significant percentage of students in introductory courses are expected to fail and leave the field has a big influence on the experiences of new undergraduates interested in a STEM major [16, 47]. In fact, the majority of all students who enter 4-year institutions intending to major in the natural sciences, technology, engineering, and mathematics do not earn a degree in these fields. Many drop out of college and others switch majors, often citing the low quality of the teaching as a major reason [46, 48]. Departmental efforts to create change can be hampered by the lack of data available to inform reform decisions. Without reliable information about where students encounter barriers, the nature of the barriers, and profiles of the students who encounter barriers, it can be difficult for leaders to determine what actions to take [16].

Comparable percentages of Black, Latino/a and White college freshmen report that they intend to major in a science or engineering field [49] and declare a STEM major [47]. However, only 43 percent of Latino/a students and 34 percent of Black students persist to earn a STEM degree compared to 58 percent of White students [47]. Of total STEM degrees awarded, approximately 9 percent went to Black graduates and 9 percent to Latino/a graduates, despite Black people comprising 14 percent and Latino/a people being 18 percent of the U.S. population [38].

Students of color are more likely to attend community colleges and 2-year private institutions, which have fewer resources than 4-year colleges [16]. In 2018, 44 percent of all Latino/a and 36 percent of all Black undergraduates attended 2-year institutions; 31 percent of all White undergraduates did [50]. Yet compared to 4-year colleges, 2-year colleges have almost $9,000 less revenue per student to devote to faculty salaries and student supports [51]. Financial issues are also relevant at the level of individual students. Black students borrow more than other students for the same degrees and are less likely to complete their degrees, so can be left with debt despite lacking the credential that could drive a higher earning potential [52, 53].

Higher education faculty are less likely to be people of color than their students. Only 24 percent are not White compared to 45 percent of students [54]. The absence of diversity among faculty at the collegiate level appears to impact learning as well, some studies indicate that students perform better when their instructors are of the same race or gender [55, 56, 57, 58]. In addition, the training of higher education faculty focuses on research rather than teaching and many incentives push them to devote more energy to research than improving their pedagogical skills and teaching strategies, reinforcing the continued use of traditional approaches to teaching. [45]

Workforce and Society

There are also broader and historic systemic inequities that make it harder for some students to have the opportunity to continue in science. We have already noted the nation's poor track record of preparing a STEM workforce that looks like the nation. Although we know that K-12 and higher education have played a role in producing disparities in STEM employment, we also acknowledge that there are historic systemic inequities outside of education that limit opportunity. **Gender inequities can be traced to past and current injustices**, including the absence of suffrage and legal protections, uneven access to education and employment opportunities, and belief systems that math and science are disciplines reserved for White men, for instance. **The racial disparities in STEM professions—like so many other racial inequities—are created by a complex set of injustices piling up on each other over centuries**, such as housing and employment discrimination and discriminatory lending practices that have denied communities of color family wealth and made it far more difficult for them to aspire to and purchase a college education [59, 60, 61].

There is already a huge income gap between White people and people of color. The U.S. Census Bureau reported on the real median household income by race and Latino/a origin in 2018 [62]. The average household income for people who are non-Latino/a White was $70,642, compared to $51,540 for people who are Latino/a of any race and $41,361 for Black people. There is also a profound gap in family wealth, particularly between White people and Black people. The Brookings Institution reports that in 2016 the net worth of the typical White family was $171,000, a figure almost 10 times higher than that of the typical Black family, with wealth of only $17,150 [63].

More, these acts of discrimination have created racially isolated communities of color, particularly in neighborhoods that are underresourced and serviced by schools that are also racially isolated and often do not offer the same educational opportunities that White students have in metropolitan communities. In fact, 70 years after Brown v. Board of Education, students of color are more likely to attend racially segregated schools. Sixty percent of Latino/a, 58 percent of Black, 53 percent of Pacific Islander, and 37% of American Indian students are enrolled in them compared to 5 percent of White students [38]. If these racially isolated communities have high levels of families experiencing poverty—and racial residential segregation and racially concentrated poverty go hand-in-hand [1, 64]—then opportunities to experience high-quality science learning are far more limited. For example, schools with the greatest percentage of students experiencing poverty are less likely to offer any physics course (90% v. 43%) than schools with the lowest percentage [30].

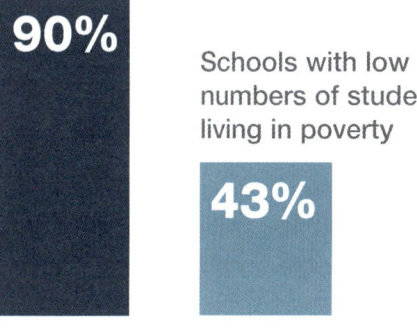

Percentage of schools offering no physics course.

On top of these systemic racial and socioeconomic inequities, people of color must confront individual and institutional biases. These biases include assumptions that they are less capable, cannot succeed in school, and are destined for low-wage professions. Biased stereotypical views about the interest or abilities of particular students or demographic groups work in both subtle and overt ways to curtail their educational experiences and result in inequitable learning supports [14]. They also impact outcomes. Recent research suggests that educators have a "slight" implicit anti-Black and pro-White bias, and in counties in which these biases are stronger, there are greater racial disparities in test scores and suspensions [65]. These factors combine to result in students of color having different learning experiences and opportunities compared to their White classmates and that in turn means that their ability to continue in science is limited in ways that contribute to current patterns of employment [6].

How Do We Get There?

The American education system is highly decentralized, a reality that presents both challenges and opportunities for a national call to action for science education. Decentralization means that there is flexibility to meet the needs of local communities and regions. However, it also means that there is no central driver for maintaining quality and ensuring equity. As a result, there are often wide disparities in access to high-quality learning experiences, well-prepared science teachers, and well-resourced institutions of higher education.

The committee calls for a national approach that energizes actors at the federal and state levels, but that honors local communities.

Recognizing this reality, the committee calls for a national approach that energizes actors at federal and state levels but that honors local communities, acknowledges the genius they bring to solving problems, and takes into account the assets they leverage to implement their plans. Examples of that genius in action are abundant in the form of alliances to improve education in municipalities and regions across the country. These kinds of alliances—focused on providing better and more equitable education experiences for students from cradle to career—are already active in communities across the country, including Buffalo, Chattanooga, Dallas, and Tacoma, as well as in larger regions such as the Rio Grande Valley [66].

While there is demonstrated capacity for alliances to form in communities to address tough challenges, still national and state leaders must use policy, public leadership, and funding streams to create incentives for the widespread implementation of high-quality more equitable science learning experiences. Federal and state action will inspire and support community efforts and initiatives to elevate and improve science that take into account the unique contexts and assets of different municipalities and regions of the country, including the formation of alliances that coordinate the activities of multiple partners to implement **better, more equitable science education.** Decades of improvement efforts and evaluation make clear that having a vision, using this vision to align policies and practices, and targeting attention to places where there is consistent lack of access to high-quality opportunities are essential strategies for improving education [14, 67]. **Developing a vision for better, more equitable science education across K-16** is an essential first step for local and state leaders who will need to work together to improve systems and practices, curriculum, instruction, and assessment.

Priorities for advancing better, more equitable science education

Our call to action highlights five priorities for communities to address as they work to improve science education and broaden opportunity in the discipline. Under each priority below we identify high-level issues and steps to take. It is beyond the scope of this report to provide detailed, step-by-step guidance. However, previous reports from the National Academies offer extensive evidence-based guidance on how to move forward (*see the section on For Further Reading*).

First, communities will need to provide the time, materials, and resources necessary to support high-quality science learning experiences for all students across the K-16 continuum.

In elementary school—starting in kindergarten—ensuring students spend sufficient time learning science each week is essential. Even the youngest children are capable of engaging in science investigations. Making science a fundamental part of K-5 instruction leverages their natural curiosity about the world. In addition, science provides a rich context for building competencies in mathematics and English/Language Arts and for developing language [68, 69, 70].

Across the K-12 continuum, districts will need to provide high-quality instructional materials and ample space for conducting investigations, and supplies [14, 17]. This might also include technology. It will be essential to identify disparities in access or resources across districts and schools or among classrooms in the same school and work to ameliorate them.

At the secondary level, students need access to the full range of science courses (biology, chemistry, physics, and Earth and space science) and advanced coursework, such as Advanced Placement, International Baccalaureate or dual enrollment programs. This will also require strategies for ensuring there are teachers who have sufficient preparation to teach these courses. Students of color and students experiencing poverty need to take these courses in equal measure and have equitable access to local and regional partnerships that provide extended learning opportunities in classrooms, through afterschool and summer programs, apprenticeships, internships, and other programs.

As students move into all types of postsecondary settings, they will need continued access to student-centered, nonlecture-based instruction, and to facilities and resources that allow frequent opportunities to conduct scientific investigations and engage in small-group discussions [15, 16]. It will also be important for postsecondary students to have access to internships, apprenticeships, and other co-curricular activities that deepen their knowledge and allow them to explore a potential STEM career or pursue a scientific passion.

Second, having a high-quality, diverse workforce for teaching science across K-16 is essential.

Teachers are the engines of **better, more equitable science education**. At every stage of the K-16 continuum, students need science teachers who both understand science and know how to teach it in engaging, student-centered ways that reflect current evidence about how people learn [15, 16, 19]. Professional development for all K-16 teachers of science is therefore essential.

Starting in preservice, K-12 teachers need opportunities to learn about, try out, and refine instructional strategies for engaging students actively in science. These instructional strategies require a different set of skills and knowledge than traditional lecture and text-based approaches, so even veteran teachers may need additional learning opportunities. Effective professional learning experiences for teachers are ongoing, closely connected to the curriculum being taught, and allow time for reflection [19]. As science is an essential literacy on par with English/Language Arts and mathematics, communities need to devote the same measure of professional development resources, including time, to science as the other disciplines. There is a particular need in postsecondary education for all who teach science (faculty, instructors, lecturers, grad students, and post docs) to have opportunities to learn about effective science pedagogy. (*See Box 7 for information on professional development for postsecondary faculty*.) All instructors of science across K-16 need to engage in ongoing learning designed to reduce reliance on lecture and increase application of student-centered instructional approaches.

Attracting and retaining more science teachers of color is a top priority for all levels of education [20]. For example, many efforts are working to strengthen pathways for more diverse people to become STEM faculty [54]. Communities need to create incentives and programs to invite Black, Latino/a and Indigenous teachers into the profession and then take intentional steps to ensure they feel welcome and valued. This will likely need to include attention to the working conditions in schools.

BOX 7: PROFESSIONAL DEVELOPMENT FOR SCIENCE TEACHING IN HIGHER EDUCATION

Local, regional, and national efforts combine to help science faculty become better teachers. Some efforts have focused on a particular discipline of science. For example, the American Chemical Society *(https://www.acs.org/content/acs/en/education/educators.html)* organizes faculty development workshops, including some targeted to new faculty, and hosts a biennial conference on chemical education. The National Institute of Scientific Teaching (https://www.nisthub.org) offers national, regional, and online institutes of varying lengths for educators with a goal of making postsecondary education more active, inclusive, and student-centered. At the institutes, expert educators share evidence-based instructional practices, focusing on active learning strategies, effective assessment development, and inclusive teaching practices. Participants engage in activities, such as reflective writing, reading, researching, discussing teaching methods and philosophy, interactive presentations, and developing teaching materials they can teach and evaluate when they return to their home institutions.

The Transforming STEM Teaching Faculty Learning Program (https://teaching.berkeley.edu/programs/transforming-stem-teaching-faculty-learning-program) is a regional program that is offered by University of California, California State University, and California Community College campuses and aims to improve student achievement in undergraduate STEM classes. The program supports interdisciplinary learning communities of faculty and offers ongoing support. It has five objectives: (1) to deepen faculty's understanding of how people learn; (2) to change teaching behavior to support student learning; (3) to engage STEM faculty in habits of reflection; (4) to nurture a tradition of continued learning about teaching; and (5) to build a faculty learning community. The 10-month program has two parts. In the first, participants examine research on how students learn and how to support that learning, experiment with new practices, and apply what they have learned by redesigning a course or portion of it. In the second part, faculty apply the research as they teach the redesigned course, learn how to observe teaching practice and provide feedback, observe videos of their peers' instruction, and reflect on their own teaching practice.

Third, students need clear, supportive pathways across grades 6-16.

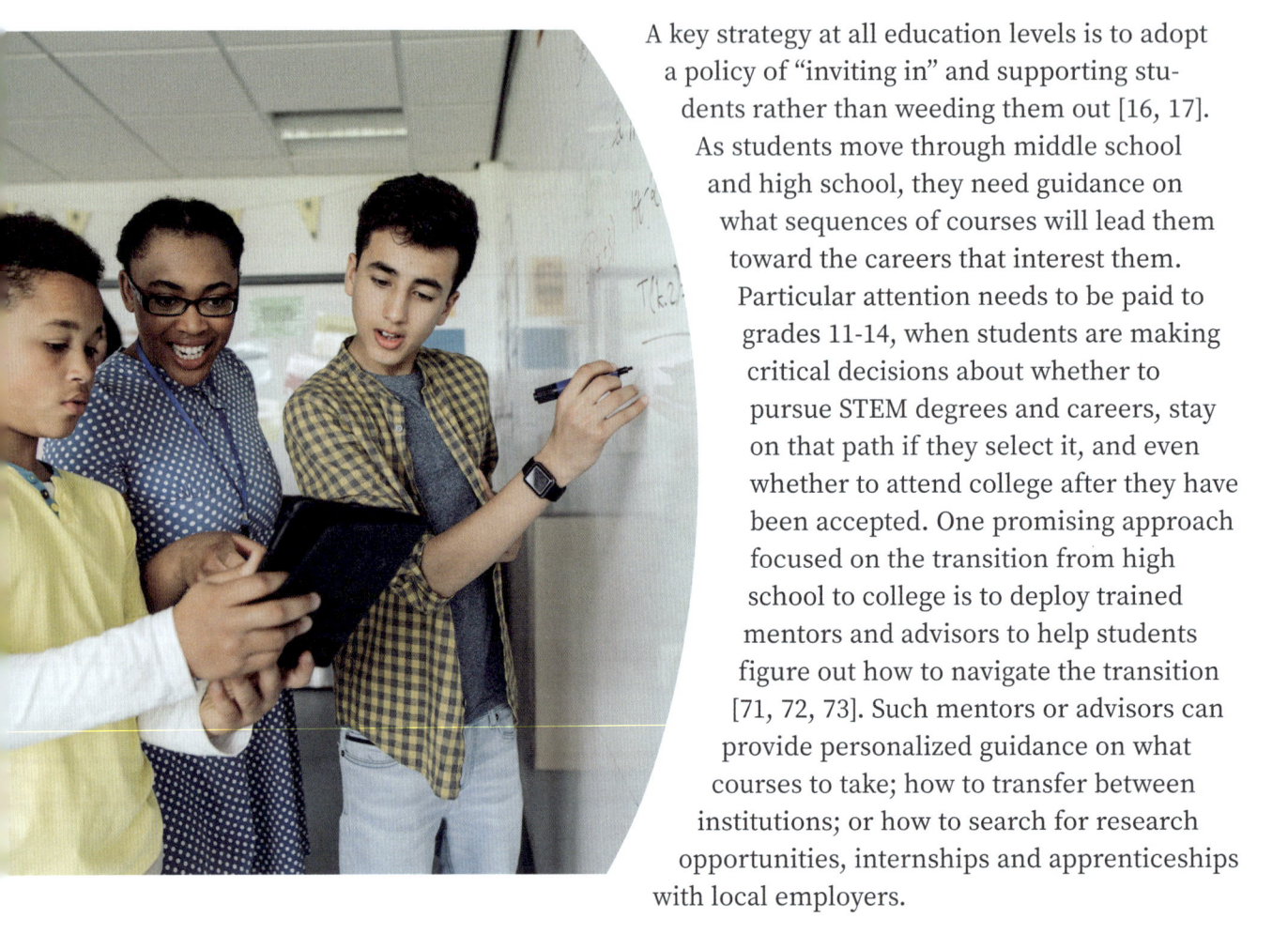

A key strategy at all education levels is to adopt a policy of "inviting in" and supporting students rather than weeding them out [16, 17]. As students move through middle school and high school, they need guidance on what sequences of courses will lead them toward the careers that interest them. Particular attention needs to be paid to grades 11-14, when students are making critical decisions about whether to pursue STEM degrees and careers, stay on that path if they select it, and even whether to attend college after they have been accepted. One promising approach focused on the transition from high school to college is to deploy trained mentors and advisors to help students figure out how to navigate the transition [71, 72, 73]. Such mentors or advisors can provide personalized guidance on what courses to take; how to transfer between institutions; or how to search for research opportunities, internships and apprenticeships with local employers.

Community colleges play a vital role in the transition from secondary to postsecondary education for many students. They are affordable and community based, their student ranks include high percentages of Black and Latino/a undergraduates, and they are essential to efforts to advance people of color along the path to STEM careers. More than 400 community colleges across the country are moving to implement guided pathways to keep students on a personalized path toward a career, including STEM professions. (*See Box 8 for further description of the guided pathways reform effort.*)

Students often take courses in multiple institutions and then have difficulty transferring their credits which may force them to repeat courses and delay their progress. States and institutions need policies that facilitate transfer of credits to

CALL TO ACTION FOR SCIENCE EDUCATION

BOX 8: GUIDED PATHWAYS TO SUPPORT STEM PROGRESSION

Guided pathways is an approach to education programming aimed at helping students develop and follow a personalized path toward a career, including STEM professions. It has been implemented by more the 400 of the nation's community colleges seeking to improve completion rates; there are also 16 statewide community college guided pathway reform efforts underway [99, 100].

This institutionwide approach to promoting students' success is based on giving students clear, coherent, and structured educational experiences that build in a variety of academic and nonacademic supports. The pathways model has four pillars of implementation:

1. Clarify the Paths
2. Help Students Get on a Path
3. Help Students Stay on Their Path
4. Ensure Students Are Learning

This approach puts equity at the center. Students' pathways guide them from their point of entry to attainment of high-quality postsecondary credentials, advancement to further education, and/or careers with value in the labor market. Having a clear end goal and following a clear pathway is expected to improve persistence and minimize excess credit hours, which waste time and money.

The model builds a range of proven practices into every student's experience, beginning with their earliest interactions with the college. These practices provide structure, help students identify their educational and career goals, and support students so they stay engaged and on track. They include

- Academic advising that incorporates in-depth conversations about career goals, degree plans, transfer opportunities, and commitments outside of college.
- Career exploration in the first academic term supported by detailed information about careers and salaries that can result from each program and credential.
- Meta-majors—groups of related majors—that provide a structure for career and academic communities.
- Gateway courses that are aligned with students' programs of study.
- Co-requisites through which underprepared students can earn college credit in their first term while getting the additional academic support they need.

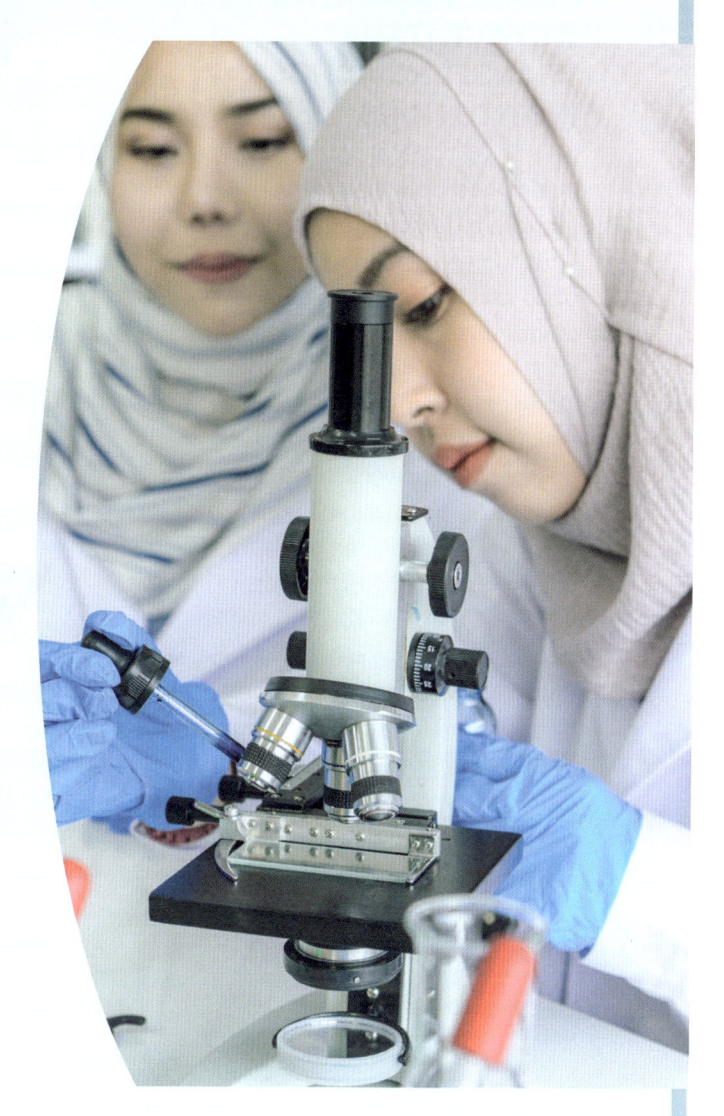

BOX 9: FLORIDA PROMOTES PATHWAYS BY FACILITATING TRANSFERS ACROSS INSTITUTIONS

Florida has state policy that requires a 36-hour general education program that is part of an associates of arts degree to introduce students to the knowledge, skills, and value of study of academic disciplines. Articulation agreements between colleges and universities guarantee that the 36-hour general education block will be accepted in full by any other public college or university in the state and that the receiving institution cannot require any other additional credits (http://www.fldoe.org/policy/articulation/). The state also employs a statewide course numbering (https://www.fgcu.edu/acs/curriculumdevelopment/files/Statewide_Course_Numbering_Guide-ADA.pdf) system to facilitate the transfer of credit across all public postsecondary institutions (*https://www.famu.edu/Architecture/Curricula/Articulation/Pathways_to_Success.pdf*). By law, the state assigns comparable courses the same prefix and number, and institutions accepting transfer students must assign credits as if the student had taken the course on their campuses.

help students stay on track and avoid running out of financial aid. (*See Box 9 for an example of state policy—in Florida—that facilitates the smooth transition for students from one higher education institution to another.*)

There are many approaches that can support students in their pathways to and through undergraduate STEM degrees. For example, many minority-serving institutions have an intentional culture of supporting students and this allows them to produce a disproportionate share of the nation's STEM undergraduates, one-fifth of the total [74]. Study of minority-serving institutions has identified effective mentorship and sponsorship, the cultivation of campus climates that respond to students' needs, mission-driven leadership, and student exposure to undergraduate research as promising approaches.

Fourth, science assessments and accountability systems need to be aligned with the vision for high-quality science instruction.

Assessing science learning in ways that are aligned to our vision will require approaches that go beyond single tests of factual knowledge. Traditional, large-scale, multiple-choice tests cannot capture the ability of students to engage in the practices of science and reason about evidence [75]. An advantage of the new approach to science instruction is that it provides many opportunities for assessing learning informally (formative assessment) as students engage in investigations, create representations, and discuss evidence [75, 76]. However, designing useful and meaningful formal assessments such as tests will require careful articulation of the desired learning goals and how students can demonstrate that they have achieved them [15, 75].

Including science more prominently in state accountability systems may help to elevate science as a priority, particularly at the elementary level. However, featuring science more prominently does not mean that states should administer a single test that checks for rote learning at the end of the school year. Rather, multiple and varied assessments designed to check for conceptual understanding and proficiency with science practices are needed. The assessments need to both inform classroom instruction and provide information about the progress of schools as well as districts and states. An assessment system for science also needs to include ways to document the distribution of high-quality science learning, K-16 across a given state to ensure that disparities in access and opportunity are identified and can be addressed [75].

Fifth, use evidence to document progress and inform ongoing improvement efforts.

As communities mobilize to address opportunity gaps in science education, they will need to use evidence to guide their efforts [1, 77, 78]. This includes data collected by school systems and institutions. Local and regional data will reveal where there are opportunity gaps (lack of resources, lack of access to advanced courses, lack of experienced science teachers) and provide a way to track progress in addressing them. Indicators to measure equity of access to high-quality science learning opportunities can include

- the amount of time elementary schools devote to science instruction each week;
- the number of science courses required for high school graduation;
- student access to rigorous science coursework and Career and Technical Education coursework grounded in science;
- qualifications and experience levels of K-12 science teachers;

- the provision of professional development opportunities for K-12 teachers and postsecondary faculty;
- the number of students who go on to postsecondary opportunities in science;
- the rates of transfer from 2- to 4-year institutions of higher education and of completion of 2- and 4-year degrees in STEM fields with particular attention to the science disciplines;
- access to internships and apprenticeships; and
- the success rate of pathway efforts and other mechanisms to promote advancement into STEM fields.

The data collected can be developed over time and start with the data that are most readily available to local K-12 school systems, postsecondary institutions, and states. Data should be disaggregated by disability status of students, gender, race, the percent of students experiencing poverty, the percentage of English language learners, and whether a school or district is in an urban, suburban, or rural area.

Working to Address the Priorities

To provide **better, more equitable science education**, leaders of local and regional K-12 systems and postsecondary institutions will need to work together with government and business, nonprofit and civic groups to develop and implement plans for improving science education that address these five priority areas. These plans can be integrated into existing strategic plans for STEM education. These collaborative efforts can drive focused, coordinated action to improve science education that are grounded in the needs of local communities and leverage local assets and stakeholder interest to help them thrive. These local and regional alliances can also elevate the importance of science in community conversations about education, the workforce, and the quality of life. Empowered local stakeholders who understand their communities' unique civic and education infrastructures, assets, and needs can marshal community resources and assets to increase opportunity for learners to engage in high-quality, science-focused learning experiences along their pathways from K-12 and into postsecondary. The plans can leverage existing opportunities in after-school programs, workplaces, museums, libraries, and parks as well as in primary, secondary, and postsecondary institutions of all types.

These alliances can examine systems, practices and expectations across K-16 systems to determine if they are serving community interest and advancing priorities, and identify where supplemental or reallocations of funds would promote improvement.

Communities can model these alliances on successful networks and initiatives, such as research practice partnerships, networked improvement communities, and collective impact initiatives [79, 80].

As the alliances move forward with their work, it will be important to ensure that the people who are closest to the work of learning and teaching are an integral part of the work: teachers, principals, district leaders, faculty (tenure, nontenure, adjunct), lecturers, department chairs, and students. Evidence shows that principals in K-12 and department chairs are especially important leaders for supporting instructional change.

The committee recognizes that these efforts will require substantial financial investments and will take time. Leaders in education, business, and in the community will need to identify potential sources of new funding and consider ways to repurpose existing funding streams. Local philanthropy has a major role to play in supporting the work. Perhaps most importantly, elevating **better, more equitable science education** and fully addressing deeply entrenched disparities in access and opportunity will take time. While small gains may be seen more quickly, fully achieving the vision we have laid out will require long-term, sustainable investments and attention over a period of at least 5 to 10 years.

Recommendations

Federal and state policy makers and national stakeholders in STEM education can play key roles in supporting the work of local and regional communities as they work to expand opportunities in science education. We outline below specific steps federal and state governments and national stakeholders can take to advance this vision for **better, more equitable science education**.

ACTION AREA 1: ELEVATE THE STATUS OF SCIENCE EDUCATION

RECOMMENDATION 1: The White House, with leadership from the Office of Science and Technology Policy (OSTP), should act to raise the profile of science education and elevate the importance of access to high-quality science learning opportunities for all students across K-16. Specifically, OSTP should encourage national stakeholders, including federal agencies, along with those in the education, business, nonprofit, scientific, and philanthropic sectors, to focus resources and leverage their assets to increase the quality of and accessibility to K-16 science education.

RECOMMENDATION 2: Congress should include science as an indicator of academic achievement when it next reauthorizes the Elementary and Secondary Education Act. Accountability for science should focus on students gaining conceptual understanding of science and should not be based on single tests. It should involve a system of assessments and indicators that together provide results that complement each other and provide information about the progress of schools, districts, and states.

RECOMMENDATION 3: State Departments of Education should act now to include science in their accountability systems for K-12 education. A state accountability system for science needs to include assessments that support classroom instruction, assessments that monitor science learning more broadly (at the school, district, and state levels), and indicators that track the availability of high-quality science learning opportunities.

CALL TO ACTION FOR SCIENCE EDUCATION

RECOMMENDATION 4: National stakeholders in science, technology, engineering, and mathematics (STEM) education should undertake coordinated advocacy to improve science education K-16 with particular attention to addressing disparities in opportunity. These stakeholders (including professional organizations, advocacy groups, scientists, and business and industry) will need to balance advocacy for STEM broadly with attention to the importance of high-quality learning experiences in science as well as in each of the other STEM disciplines.

A shared call to action and mutually reinforcing activities by the many diverse groups active in the promotion of science and STEM education is essential to the implementation of the recommendations presented in this report. Coordinated efforts and a common voice rather than siloed initiatives and disparate messaging can elevate science education to a level of importance in national, state and local discourse about K-16 education. All stakeholders can come to agreement on the importance of helping the American public understand that science education is essential to creating well-informed communities and preparing future workers for STEM and other careers and that states, systems, and institutions should be held accountable for closing opportunity gaps that exist in science education. Stakeholders can therefore share consistent messages and coordinate efforts to help bring about change on local, regional, and national levels.

ACTION AREA 2: ESTABLISH LOCAL AND REGIONAL ALLIANCES FOR STEM OPPORTUNITY

RECOMMENDATION 5: Leaders of local and regional K-12 systems and postsecondary institutions should work together to form Alliances for STEM Opportunity that involve key stakeholders in science, technology, engineering, and mathematics (STEM) education, such as informal education organizations, nonprofits, afterschool and summer programs, business and industry, and the philanthropic sector. Each alliance should develop an evidence-based vision and plan for improving STEM education that includes specific attention to high-quality science learning opportunities and addresses disparities in opportunity. Plans should include, at minimum, strategies for:

(1) providing access to high-quality science learning experiences across K-16 and addressing existing disparities in access;
(2) providing high-quality instructional materials and other resources to support these experiences;
(3) building a high-quality, diverse workforce for teaching science to include provisions for professional development and ongoing support;
(4) creating pathways for learners in science across grades 6 through 16 with supports for learners who want to pursue STEM careers.

RECOMMENDATION 6: The federal government, philanthropic organizations, and business and industry should provide funding to support the work of local and regional Alliances for STEM Opportunity as they work to improve science education. Funding should be targeted first to communities where a significant number of students live in poverty. Funds should support coordination and management of the alliances, programmatic efforts, and research and evaluation.

Alliances can be the linchpin of efforts to advance better and more equitable science experiences in communities. Their members can work together to identify the most appropriate shared priorities and then determine which approaches to science education will best serve local interests. They can rally stakeholders to elevate the importance of science education, develop plans, set priorities, collect and synthesize data to measure progress, make adjustments to strategies based on evidence, and hold partners accountable. Members of an alliance can work towards a common vision in ways that leverage what they do best. For example, some alliance members might provide programming while others collect or disseminate data, mobilize parents, provide high school or college counseling or advocate, all in service to goals and strategies jointly set by the alliance's members.

Existing local, regional, or national networks focused on STEM, such as the STEM ecosystems, can catalyze, join or contribute to the Alliances for STEM Opportunity. Our intent is not to supplant existing efforts, but to ensure that there is attention to the quality and equity of science education specifically and to each of the STEM disciplines individually.

That federal and philanthropic funding for alliances targets underresourced communities and schools is especially important for addressing existing disparities in access and opportunity. Processes for alliances to secure funding will need to be structured to ensure all communities have equitable opportunities to apply for and receive financial support. Funding provided by the National Science Foundation could be focused on documenting through research and evaluation the approaches that are most improving science education overall and eliminating disparities in opportunity and outcomes.

ACTION AREA 3: DOCUMENT PROGRESS TOWARD BETTER, MORE EQUITABLE SCIENCE EDUCATION

RECOMMENDATION 7: States should develop and implement data-driven state-level plans for providing equitable K-16 science, technology, engineering, and mathematics (STEM) education with specific attention to science. These plans should include "STEM Opportunity Maps" that document and track where opportunities are available, where there are disparities in opportunity, and how much progress is being made toward eliminating disparities and achieving the goals of the state STEM education plan. The STEM Opportunity Maps should incorporate documentation from local and regional Alliances for STEM Opportunity.

RECOMMENDATION 8: The federal government should develop an annual "STEM Opportunity in the States" report card that documents the status of K-16 science, technology, engineering, and mathematics (STEM) education across each of the states and territories and tracks equity of opportunity for students in science specifically and in each of the other STEM disciplines.

Gathering and evaluating data about the distribution and quality of science learning experiences will provide decision makers with information they can use to identify disparities, track efforts to improve and direct resources to where they are needed most [81, 82]. States needs to be held accountable by a range of stakeholders for whether they are improving science education and closing opportunity gaps in science.

There are current federal programs that track information state by state and present it in an annual report, such as the Department of Education's Civil Rights Data Collection[3] or the National Science Foundation for its Science and Engineering State Profiles.[4] These programs may offer models of how to obtain data from states, and manage, analyze and report it. Within states themselves, there are numerous examples of data-tracking in education that could be either modified or supplemented to include information on science and STEM without creating significant additional administrative burden.

---

[3]For more information, see https://ocrdata.ed.gov/.
[4]For more information, see https://www.nsf.gov/statistics/states/#ui-id-4.

How Can We Learn from These Efforts?

Implementation of this Call to Action presents the opportunity to elevate the importance of science education across the country. It could also be a tremendous opportunity to document the work of the Alliances for STEM Opportunity and learn from them. Researchers, educators, and other stakeholders can study how the alliances develop and act on strategies to improve science learning, and on how they create more coherent and equitable science learning opportunities across K-12, postsecondary, and in the community. Specific attention to entrenched disparities in access and opportunity can provide important lessons for addressing the broader, long-standing inequities in the American educational system K-16.

While the evidence base the committee drew on to develop this Call to Action is broad and deep, there are still many questions that can only be answered with more evidence. For instance, what strategies are most effective for advancing change in educational institutions in ways that center equity? How does context affect which strategies work best? How can better strategies for supporting science teacher learning across K-16 be designed and implemented, beginning in pre service for K-12 and when postsecondary faculty are in graduate school? What are novel funding models for science education in K-12 and postsecondary that ensure resources are distributed to schools, school systems, and institutions that serve students who are most in need? How can technology be used to support learning in science in equitable ways?

In Conclusion

As a committee, we have planted a stake firmly in the ground in this national call to action for **better, more equitable science education**. We ask federal and state policy makers, philanthropies, and local communities to plant stakes next to our own and say in a unified voice that science education is a national priority because it is essential to our nation's vitality, the maintenance of its democracy, the quality of life its people lead, the health of its economy and its ability to respond to big challenges like the COVID-19 pandemic. Concerted and coordinated action at national, state, and local levels consistent with the recommendations we lay out must follow.

We earlier noted that we developed the content and the recommendations of this report in the midst of the pandemic as well as a national reckoning on race. Both the spread of COVID-19 and historic inequities based on race and income have ravaged communities from coast to coast, in regions such as Appalachia, the Old Plantation South, and the Rio Grande Valley of Texas and in cities from Buffalo to Dallas to Los Angeles. However, we believe that the nation has an opportunity to reset the way it delivers or supports the delivery of what the American people need to thrive —including how the nation's schools and communities deliver science education.

The pandemic has reminded the nation how important science is, not only in providing a way out of it through the quick production of vaccines but also in demonstrating why everyone living in America must understand the basics of science. The national reckoning on race has elevated historic inequities in, among other areas, health, employment, and education. That reckoning has made clear that addressing these inequities must be a national priority as well. The nation has an opportunity to reset science education so that it is **better** for all Americans and **more equitable** for populations of students from rural communities and those who are of color or are experiencing poverty. America needs **better, more equitable science education.** We know America can deliver it.

References

1. National Academies of Sciences, Engineering, and Medicine. (2019). *Monitoring Educational Equity*. Washington, DC: The National Academies Press. https://doi.org/10.17226/25389.

2. National Academies of Sciences, Engineering, and Medicine. (2016). *Science Literacy: Concepts, Contexts, and Consequences*. Washington, DC: The National Academies Press. https://doi.org/10.17226/23595.

3. Cherrstrom, C.A., Lopez, O.S., and Ashford-Hanserd, S. (2021). STEM Knowledge in Non-STEM Occupations: Implications for Community Colleges, *Community College Journal of Research and Practice*, DOI: 10.1080/10668926.2020.1868359.

4. U.S. Bureau of Labor Stats. Available: https://www.bls.gov/emp/tables/stem-employment.htm.

5. National Science Board, National Science Foundation. (2018). *Science and Engineering Indicators 2018*. NSB-2018-1. Available: https://www.nsf.gov/statistics/2018/nsb20181/.

6. National Academies of Sciences, Engineering, and Medicine. (2011). *Expanding Underrepresented Minority Participation: America's Science and Technology Talent at the Crossroads*. Washington, DC: The National Academies Press. https://doi.org/10.17226/12984.

7. Cohen, J.J., Gabriel, B.A., and Terrell, C. (2002). The case for diversity in the health care workforce. *Health Affairs (Project Hope)*, *21*(5), 90–102.

8. Federal Glass Ceiling Commission. (1995). *Good for Business: Making Full Use of the Nation's Human Capital*. U.S. Department of Labor. Available: https://ecommons.cornell.edu/handle/1813/79348.

9. Florida, R. (2014). *The Rise of the Creative Class—Revisited: Revised and Expanded.* New York: Basic Books.

10. Centre for Strategy and Evaluation Services. (2003). *The Costs and Benefits of Diversity: A Study on Methods and Indicators to Measure the Cost Effectiveness of Diversity Policies in Enterprises: Executive summary. European Commission.* Available: https://www.coe.int/t/dg4/cultureheritage/mars/source/resources/references/others/17%20-%20Costs%20and%20Benefits%20of%20Diversity%20-%20EU%202003%20ExSum.pdf.

11. Campbell, L.G., Mehtani, S., Dozier, M.E., and Rinehart, R. (2013). Gender-heterogeneous working groups produce higher quality science. *PLOS ONE 8*(10).

12. National Academies of Sciences, Engineering, and Medicine. (2018). *How People Learn II: Learners, Contexts, and Cultures*. Washington, DC: The National Academies Press. https://doi.org/10.17226/24783.

13. National Research Council. (2007). *Taking Science to School: Learning and Teaching Science in Grades K-8*. Washington, DC: The National Academies Press. https://doi.org/10.17226/11625.

14. Arum, N., Besley, J., and Gomez, L. (2018). Disparities in Science Literacy. *Science, 360*(6391), 861-862. DOI: 10.1126/science.aar8480.

15. National Research Council. (2012). *A Framework for K-12 Science Education: Practices, Crosscutting Concepts, and Core Ideas*. Washington, DC: The National Academies Press. https://doi.org/10.17226/13165.

16. National Research Council. (2012). *Discipline-Based Education Research: Understanding and Improving Learning in Undergraduate Science and Engineering.* Washington, DC: The National Academies Press. https://doi.org/10.17226/13362.

17. National Academies of Sciences, Engineering, and Medicine. (2016). *Barriers and Opportunities for 2-Year and 4-Year STEM Degrees: Systemic Change to Support Students' Diverse Pathways.* Washington, DC: The National Academies Press. https://doi.org/10.17226/21739.

18. National Academies of Sciences, Engineering, and Medicine. (2019). *Science and Engineering for Grades 6-12: Investigation and Design at the Center.* Washington, DC: The National Academies Press. https://doi.org/10.17226/25216.

19. National Academies of Sciences, Engineering, and Medicine. (2015). *Science Teachers' Learning: Enhancing Opportunities, Creating Supportive Contexts.* Washington, DC: The National Academies Press. https://doi.org/10.17226/21836.

20. National Academies of Sciences, Engineering, and Medicine. (2020). *Changing Expectations for the K-12 Teacher Workforce: Policies, Preservice Education, Professional Development, and the Workplace.* Washington, DC: The National Academies Press. https://doi.org/10.17226/25603.

21. Ong, M., Wright, C., Espinosa, L. L., and Orfield, G. (2011). Inside the double bind: A synthesis of empirical research on undergraduate and graduate women of color in science, technology, engineering, and mathematics. *Harvard Educational Review, 81*(2), 172–208. https://doi.org/10.17763/haer.81.2.t022245n7x4752v2.

22. National Academies of Sciences, Engineering, and Medicine. (2018). *Sexual Harassment of Women: Climate, Culture, and Consequences in Academic Sciences, Engineering, and Medicine.* Washington, DC: The National Academies Press. https://doi.org/10.17226/24994.

23. National Academies of Sciences, Engineering, and Medicine. (2020). *Promising Practices for Addressing the Underrepresentation of Women in Science, Engineering, and Medicine: Opening Doors.* Washington, DC: The National Academies Press. https://doi.org/10.17226/25585.

24. National Academies of Sciences, Engineering, and Medicine. (2017). *Undergraduate Research Experiences for STEM Students: Successes, Challenges, and Opportunities.* Washington, DC: The National Academies Press. https://doi.org/10.17226/24622.

25. National Center for Education Statistics, U.S. Department of Education. (2017). *The Nation's Report Card: 2015 Science at Grades 4, 8 and 12.* NCES 2016162. Available: https://nces.ed.gov/pubsearch/pubsinfo.asp?pubid=2016162.

26. Horizon Research, Inc. (2019). *Highlights from the 2018 NSSME+.* Available: http://www.horizon-research.com/highlights-from-the-2018-nssme.

27. Blank, R.K. (2013). Science instructional time is declining in elementary schools: What are the implications for student achievement and closing the gap?. *Science Education, 97*(6), 830–847.

28. Judson, E. (2013). The relationship between time allocated for science in elementary schools and state accountability policies. *Science Education,* 97(4), 621–636.

29. Hartry, A., Dorph, R., Shields, P., Tiffany-Morales, J., and Romero, V. (2012). *The Status of Middle School Science Education in California.* Sacramento, CA: The Center for the Future of Teaching and Learning at WestEd.

30. Change the Equation. (2017). *Ending the Double Disadvantage: Ensuring STEM Opportunities in Our Poorest Schools.* Available: https://www.ecs.org/wp-content/uploads/CTE_STEM-Desert-Brief_FINAL.pdf.

31. Banilower, E.R., Smith, P.S., Weiss, I.R., Malzahn, K.A., Campbell, K.M., and Weis, A.M. (2013). *Report of the 2012 National Survey of Science and Mathematics Education.* Horizon Research, Inc. Available: http://www.horizon-research.com/2012nssme/wp-content/uploads/2013/02/2012-NSSME-Full-Report1.pdf.

32. National Academies of Sciences, Engineering, and Medicine. (2020). *Reopening K-12 Schools During the COVID-19 Pandemic: Prioritizing Health, Equity, and Communities.* Washington, DC: The National Academies Press. https://doi.org/10.17226/25858.

33. Trygstad, P.J., Malzahn, K.A., Banilower, E.R., Plumley, C.L., and Bruce, A.D. (2020). *Are All Students Getting Equal Access to High-Quality Science Education? Data from the 2018 NSSME+.* Horizon Research, Inc. Available: http://www.horizon-research.com/horizonresearchwp/wp-content/uploads/2020/11/Equity_Science_FINAL.pdf.

34. Dee, T.S. and Goldhaber, D. (2017). *Understanding and Addressing Teacher Shortages in the United States.* The Hamilton Project, Brookings. Policy Proposal 2017-05.

35. https://nces.ed.gov/programs/coe/indicator/clr.

36. Egalite, A., and Kisida, B. (2017). The effects of teacher match on students' academic perceptions and attitudes. *Educational Evaluation and Policy Analysis. 40*(1), 59–81. https://doi.org/10.3102/0162373717714056.

37. Ingersoll, R., May, H., and Collins, G. (2019). Recruitment, employment, retention, and the minority teacher shortage. *Education Policy Analysis Archives, 27*(37). http://dx.doi.org/10.14507/epaa.27.3714.

38. de Brey, C., Musu, L., McFarland, J., Wilkinson-Flicker, S., Diliberti, M., Zhang, A., Branstetter, C., and Wang, X. (2019). *Status and Trends in the Education of Racial and Ethnic Groups 2018.* NCES 2019-038. National Center for Education Statistics, U.S. Department of Education. Available: https://nces.ed.gov/pubs2019/2019038.pdf.

39. ExcelinEd. (2018). *College and Career Pathways: Equity and Access.* Available: https://www.excelined.org/wp-content/uploads/2018/10/ExcelinEd.Report.CollegeCareerPathways.CRDCAnalysis.2018.pdf.

40. ECS/College Board. Advanced-Placement-Access-and-Success-How-do-rural-schools-stack-up.pdf (ecs.org).

41. Gao, N. (2016). *College Readiness in California: A Look at Rigorous High School Course-Taking.* Public Policy Institute of California. Available: https://www.ppic.org/content/pubs/report/R_0716NGR.pdf.

42. Castleman, B., and Page, L. (2013). A trickle or a torrent? Understanding the extent of summer "melt" among college-intending high school graduates. *Social Science Quarterly, 95*(1), 202–220.

43. Hillman, N., and Weichman, T. (2016). *Education Deserts: The Continued Significance of "Place" in the Twenty-First Century. Viewpoints: Voices from the Field.* Washington, DC: American Council on Education.

44. Klasik, D., Blagg, K., and Pekor, Z. (2018). *Out of the Education Desert: How Limited Local College Options are Associated with Inequity in Postsecondary Opportunities* (CEPA Working Paper No.18-15). Available: http://cepa.stanford.edu/wp18-15.

45. M. Stains, et al. (2018). Anatomy of STEM teaching in North American universities. *Science, 359*(6383), 1468–1470. https://doi.org/10.1126/science.aap8892.

46. Seymour, E., and Hunter, A.-B. (Eds.). (2019). *Talking About Leaving Revisited: Persistence, Relocation, and Loss in Undergraduate STEM Education.* Cham, Switzerland: Springer.

47. Riegle-Crumb, C., King, B., and Irizarry, Y. (2019). Does STEM stand out? Examining racial/ethnic gaps in persistence across postsecondary fields. *Educational Researcher, 48*(3), 133–144. (Original DOI: 10.3102/0013189X19831006).

48. President's Council of Advisors on Science and Technology. (2012). *Engage to Excel: Producing One Million Additional College Graduates with Degrees in Science, Technology, Engineering, and Mathematics.* Available: https://obamaWhitehouse.archives.gov/sites/default/files/microsites/ostp/pcast-engage-to-excel-final_2-25-12.pdf.

49. National Center for Science and Engineering Statistics, National Science Foundation. (2019). *Women, Minorities, and Persons with Disabilities in Science and Engineering: 2019.* Special Report NSF 19-304. Available at https://www.nsf.gov/statistics/wmpd.

50. Snyder, T.D., de Brey, C., and Dillow, S.A. (2019). *Digest of Education Statistics 2018.* NCES 2020-009. National Center for Education Statistics, U.S. Department of Education. Available: https://nces.ed.gov/pubs2020/2020009.pdf.

51. Yuen, V. (October, 2020). *The $78 Billion Community College Funding Shortfall. Center for American Progress.* Available: https://www.americanprogress.org/issues/education-postsecondary/reports/2020/10/07/491242/78-billion-community-college-funding-shortfall/.

52. Goldrick-Rab, S., Kelchen, R., and Houle, J. (2014). *Color of Student Debt: Implications of Federal Loan Program Reforms for Black Students and Historically Black Colleges and Universities.* Wisconsin Hope Lab. Paper for discussion.

53. Scott-Clayton, J., and Li, J. (2016). Black-White disparity in student loan debt more than triples after graduation. *Evidence Speaks Reports, 2* (3). Brookings.

54. National Center for Education Statistics, U.S. Department of Education. (2018). *Digest of Education Statistics.* Available: https://nces.ed.gov/programs/digest/2018menu_tables.asp.

55. Bettinger, E., and Long, B. (2005). Do faculty serve as role models? The impact of instructor gender on women students. *American Economic Review Papers and Proceedings, 95*(2), 152-157.

56. Fairlee, R., Hoffman, F., and Oreopoulous, P. (2014). A community college instructor like me: Race and ethnicity interactions in the classroom. *American Economic Review, 104*(8), 2567–2591.

57. Hoffmann, F. and P. Oreopoulos. (2009). A professor like me: the influence of instructor gender on university achievement. *Journal of Human Resources, 44*(2), 479-494.

58. Price, J. (2010). The effect of instructor race and gender on student persistence in STEM fields, Economics of Education Review, *29*(6), 901-910. https://doi.org/10.1016/j.econedurev.2010.07.009.

59. Addo, F.R. and Houle, J.N., and Simon, D. (2016). Young, Black, and (still) in the red: Parental wealth, race, and student loan debt, Race and Social Problems, 8(1), 64–76.

60. National Academies of Sciences, Engineering, and Medicine. (2019). *A Roadmap to Reducing Child Poverty.* Washington, DC: The National Academies Press. https://doi.org/10.17226/25246.

61. Quillian, L., Lee, J.J. and Honoré, B. (2020). Racial discrimination in the U.S. housing and mortgage lending markets: A quantitative review of trends, 1976–2016. *Race and Social Problems, 12*, 13–28. https://doi.org/10.1007/s12552-019-09276-x.

62. Semega, J., Kollar, M. Creamer, J., and Mohanty, A. (2019). *Income and Poverty in the United States: 2018-Current Population Reports.* Report number P60-266. https://www.census.gov/library/visualizations/2019/demo/p60-266.html.

63. McIntosh, K., Moss, E., Nunn, R., and Shambaugh, J. (2020). *Examining the Black White Wealth Gap.* Brookings. https://www.brookings.edu/blog/up-front/2020/02/27/examining-the-black-White-wealth-gap/.

64. Greene, S., Austin Turner, M., and Gourevitch, R. (August, 2017). *Racial Residential Segregation and Neighborhood Disparities.* U.S. Partnership on Mobility and Poverty. Available: https://www.mobilitypartnership.org/publications/racial-residential-segregation-and-neighborhood-disparities.

65. Chin, M.J., Quinn, D.M., and Dhaliwal, T.K. (2020). Bias in the air: A Nationwide exploration of teachers' implicit racial attitudes, aggregate bias, and student outcomes. *Educational Researcher, 49*(8), 566–578. https://doi.org/10.3102/0013189X20937240.

66. *We Refuse to Lose*, Education First. www.werfusetolose.org/about.

67. National Research Council. (2015). *Guide to Implementing the Next Generation Science Standards.* Washington, DC: The National Academies Press. https://doi.org/10.17226/18802.

68. Bustamante, A.S., Greenfield, D.B., and Nayfield, I. (2018). Early childhood science and engineering: Engaging platforms for fostering domain-general learning skills. *Journal of Education Sciences, 8*(3), 144-157.

69. Cervetti, G.N., Wright, T.S., and Hwang, H. (2016). Conceptual coherence, comprehension and vocabulary acquisition: A knowledge effect? *Reading and Writing*, 29, 761-779.

70. Pearson, P.D., Moje, E., and Greenleaf, C. (2010). Literacy and science: Each in the service of the other. *Science, 328*(5977), 459-463.

71. Hurd, N. M., Tan, J., Loeb, E. L. (2016). Natural mentoring relationships and the adjustment to college among underrepresented students. *American Journal of Community Psychology.*

72. Sally Lindsay, De-Lawrence Lamptey, Elaine Cagliostro, Dilakshan Srikanthan, Neda Mortaji and Leora Karon. (2019). A systematic review of postsecondary transition interventions for youth with disabilities, *Disability and Rehabilitation,* 41(21), 2492-2505, DOI: 10.1080/09638288.2018.1470260.

73. National Academies of Sciences, Engineering, and Medicine. (2019). *The Science of Effective Mentorship in STEMM.* Washington, DC: The National Academies Press. https://doi.org/10.17226/25568.

74. National Academies of Sciences, Engineering, and Medicine. (2019). *Minority-Serving Institutions: America's Underutilized Resource for Strengthening the STEM Workforce.* Washington, DC: The National Academies Press. https://doi.org/10.17226/25257.

75. National Research Council. (2014). D*eveloping Assessments for the Next Generation Science Standards.* Washington, DC: The National Academies Press. https://doi.org/10.17226/18409.

76. National Research Council. (2001). *Knowing What Students Know: The Science and Design of Educational Assessment.* Washington, DC: The National Academies Press. https://doi.org/10.17226/10019.

77. National Research Council. (2013). *Monitoring Progress Toward Successful K-12 STEM Education: A Nation Advancing?* Washington, DC: The National Academies Press. https://doi.org/10.17226/13509.

78. National Academies of Sciences, Engineering, and Medicine. (2018). *Indicators for Monitoring Undergraduate STEM Education.* Washington, DC: The National Academies Press. https://doi.org/10.17226/24943.

79. Coburn, C.E., and Penuel, W.R. (2016). Research–practice partnerships in education: Outcomes, dynamics, and open questions. *Educational Researcher, 45*(1), 48-54. https://doi.org/ 10.3102/0013189X16631750.

80. Russell, J. L., Bryk, A. S., Dolle, J. R., Gomez, L. M., L., P. G., and Grunow, A. (2017). A framework for the initiation of networked improvement communities, *Teachers College Record, 119*(5), 1-36.

81. Government Accounting Office (2016). *K-12 Education: Better Use of Information Could Help Agencies Identify Disparities and Address Racial Discrimination.* GAO-16-345. Published: Apr 21, 2016. Publicly Released: May 17, 2016. https://www.gao.gov/products/gao-16-345.

82. National Academies of Sciences, Engineering, and Medicine. (2020). *Building Educational Equity Indicator Systems: A Guidebook for States and School Districts.* Washington, DC: The National Academies Press. https://doi.org/10.17226/25833.

83. White, K., Beach, A., Finkelstein, N., Henderson, C., Simkins, S., Slakey, L., Stains, M., Weaver, G., and Whitehead, L. (Eds.). (2020). *Transforming Institutions: Accelerating Systemic Change in Higher Education.* Pressbooks. http://openbooks.library.umass.edu/ascnti2020/.

84. https://www.aacu.org/pkal.

85. https://www.aau.edu/education-community-impact.

86. https://www.aapt.org/Resources/colluniv.cfm.

87. https://visionandchange.org/resources/.

88. https://serc.carleton.edu/index.html.

89. https://serc.carleton.edu/curenet/index.html.

90. https://bayviewalliance.org.

91. https://www.cirtl.net/about.

92. https://serc.carleton.edu/integrate/index.html.

93. Ball, P. (2021). The lightning-fast quest for COVID vaccines — and what it means for other diseases. *Nature 589*, 16-18. https://doi.org/10.1038/d41586-020-03626-1.

94. https://www.washingtonpost.com/climate-environment/2020/05/06/kizzmekia-corbett-vaccine-coronavirus/.

95. https://www.cbsnews.com/news/covid-19-vaccine-development-kizzmekia-corbett/.

96. https://healthtalk.unchealthcare.org/kizzy-goes-to-sri-lanka/.

97. https://www.edc.org/igniting-rural-stem.

98. https://www.theatlantic.com/education/archive/2014/11/the-challenge-of-being-a-rural-science-teacher/382309/.

99. https://ccrc.tc.columbia.edu/publications/policy-brief-guided-pathways.html.

100. https://cccse.org/sites/default/files/BuildingMomentum.pdf.

For Further Reading

The reports listed below provide additional guidance related to moving the recommendations in this report forward and addressing the five priorities for providing **better, more equitable science education**. They are available online for free.

K-12 EDUCATION

A Framework for K-12 Science Education: Practices, Crosscutting Concepts, and Core Ideas **(2012)**
https://www.nap.edu/catalog/13165/a-framework-for-k12-science-education-practices-crosscutting-concepts

This report outlines a broad set of expectations for students in science and engineering in grades K-12. It lays out three key dimensions for learning: crosscutting concepts that unify the study of science through their common application across science and engineering; scientific and engineering practices; and disciplinary core ideas in the physical sciences, life sciences, and earth and space sciences and for engineering, technology, and the applications of science. It also discusses key issues related to improving science education including equity, curriculum and instruction, professional learning for teachers and assessment.

Guide to Implementing the Next Generation Science Standards **(2015)**
https://www.nap.edu/catalog/18802/guide-to-implementing-the-next-generation-science-standards

The *Framework* was used as a blueprint for the development of The Next Generation Science Standards, which were developed by a consortium of states. Implementing these standards and achieving the vision of the *Framework* requires time, resources, and ongoing commitment from state, district, and school leaders, as well as classroom teachers. This report identifies overarching principles that should guide the planning and implementation process that will include changes to curriculum, instruction, professional learning for teachers and administrators, policies, and assessment needed to align with the new standards.

Science and Engineering in Grades 6-12: Investigation and Design at the Center **(2018)**
https://www.nap.edu/catalog/25216/science-and-engineering-for-grades-6-12-investigation-and-design

This report provides evidence-based guidance for teachers, administrators, creators of instructional resources, and leaders of teacher professional learning on how to support students as they make sense of phenomena, gather and analyze data/information, construct explanations and design solutions, and communicate reasoning to self and others during science investigation and engineering design. It also provides guidance to help educators get started with designing, implementing, and assessing investigation and design.

Science and Engineering in Preschool Through the Elementary Grades **(Forthcoming in 2021)**

This report will provide evidence-based guidance on effective approaches to preK-5 science and engineering instruction that supports the success of all students. The report will examine the state of the evidence on learning experiences prior to school; describe promising instructional approaches across preK-5 and discuss what is needed for implementation to include teacher professional development, curriculum, and instructional materials; and the policies and practices at all levels that constrain or facilitate efforts to enhance preK-5 science and engineering.

English Learners in STEM Subjects: Transforming Classrooms, Schools, and Lives **(2018)**
https://www.nap.edu/catalog/25182/english-learners-in-stem-subjects-transforming-classrooms-schools-and-lives

The report offers guidance on how to improve learning outcomes in STEM for students who are English Learners (ELs). It considers the complex social and academic use of language delineated in the new mathematics and science standards, the diversity of the population of ELs, and the integration of English-as-a-second-language instruction with core instructional programs in STEM.

Science Teachers' Learning: Enhancing Opportunities, Creating Supportive Contexts **(2015)**
https://www.nap.edu/catalog/21836/science-teachers-learning-enhancing-opportunities-creating-supportive-contexts

This report outlines the learning needs of teachers as they work to implement new, evidence-based approaches to science education. It provides guidance for schools and districts on how best to support teachers' learning and how to implement successful programs for professional development for educators that reinforce and expand their knowledge of the major ideas and concepts in science, their familiarity with a range of instructional strategies, and the skills to implement those strategies in the classroom.

Changing Expectations for the K-12 Teacher Workforce: Policies, Preservice Education, Professional Development, and the Workplace (2020)
https://www.nap.edu/catalog/25603/changing-expectations-for-the-k-12-teacher-workforce-policies-preservice

This report explores the impact of the changing landscape of K-12 education and the potential for expansion of effective models, programs, and practices for teacher education and professional development. This report examines changing expectations for teaching and learning, trends and developments in the teacher labor market, preservice teacher education, and opportunities for learning in the workplace and in-service professional development.

Developing Assessments for the Next Generation Science Standards (2015)
https://www.nap.edu/catalog/18409/developing-assessments-for-the-next-generation-science-standards

Assessments are tools for tracking what and how well students have learned. They should be designed to support classroom instruction, monitor science learning on a broader scale, and track opportunity to learn. This report recommends strategies for developing assessments that yield valid measures of student proficiency in science; it offers a systems approach to science assessment, in which a range of assessment strategies are designed to answer different kinds of questions with appropriate degrees of specificity and provide results that complement one another.

Seeing Students Learn Science: Integrating Assessment and Instruction into the Classroom (2017)
https://www.nap.edu/catalog/23548/seeing-students-learn-science-integrating-assessment-and-instruction-in-the

This guide, based on the report *Developing Assessments for the Next Generation Science Standards*, is designed to help educators improve their understanding of how students learn science and guide the adaptation of their instruction and approach to assessment. It includes examples of innovative assessment formats, ways to embed assessments in engaging classroom activities, and ideas for interpreting and using novel kinds of assessment information. It provides ideas and questions educators can use to reflect on what they can adapt right away and what they can work toward more gradually.

Successful K-12 STEM Education: Identifying Effective Approaches in Science, Technology, Engineering and Mathematics (2011)
https://www.nap.edu/catalog/13158/successful-k-12-stem-education-identifying-effective-approaches-in-science

This report examines the landscape of K-12 STEM education by considering different school models, highlighting research on effective education practices, and identifying conditions that promote and limit school- and student-level success in the STEM subjects. It identifies three important goals that share certain elements: learning STEM content and practices, developing positive dispositions toward STEM, and preparing students to be lifelong learners.

STEM Integration in K-12 STEM Education (2014)
https://www.nap.edu/catalog/18612/stem-integration-in-k-12-education-status-prospects-and-an

This report examines efforts to connect the STEM disciplines in K-12 education. It identifies and characterizes existing approaches to integrated STEM education, both in formal and after- and out-of-school settings. The report reviews the evidence for the impact of integrated approaches on various student outcomes, and proposes a framework to provide a common perspective and vocabulary for researchers, practitioners, and others to identify, discuss, and investigate specific integrated STEM initiatives within the K-12 education system of the United States.

Monitoring Progress Toward Successful K-12 STEM Education (2013)
https://www.nap.edu/catalog/13509/monitoring-progress-toward-successful-k-12-stem-education-a-nation

This report identifies methods for tracking progress toward the recommendations of the 2011 *Successful K-12 STEM Education* report by presenting a framework and key indicators for a national-level monitoring and reporting system that could measure student knowledge, interest, and participation in the STEM disciplines and STEM-related activities; track financial, human capital, and material investments in K-12 STEM education at the federal, state, and local levels; provide information about the capabilities of the STEM education workforce, including teachers and principals; and facilitate strategic planning for federal investments in STEM education and workforce development when used with labor force projections.

***Monitoring Educational Equity* (2019)**
https://www.nap.edu/catalog/25389/monitoring-educational-equity

This report proposes a system of indicators of educational equity, presents recommendations for implementation, and serves as a framework to help policy makers better understand and combat inequity in the United States' education system. Measures of educational equity often fail to account for the impact that the circumstances in which students live have on their academic engagement, academic progress, and educational attainment. Some of the contextual factors that bear on learning include food and housing insecurity, exposure to violence, unsafe neighborhoods, adverse childhood experiences, and exposure to environmental toxins.

***Building Educational Equity Indicator Systems: A Guidebook for States School Districts* (2020)**
https://www.nap.edu/catalog/25833/building-educational-equity-indicator-systems-a-guidebook-for-states-and

The guidebook expands on the indicators of educational equity identified in the report, *Monitoring Educational Equity*, to show education leaders how they can measure educational equity within their states and school districts. For each indicator of educational equity identified in the report, the guidebook describes what leaders should measure and what data to use, provides examples of data collection instruments, and offers considerations and challenges to keep in mind.

POSTSECONDARY

***Discipline-Based Education Research: Understanding and Improving Learning in Undergraduate Science and Engineering* (2012)**
https://www.nap.edu/catalog/13362/discipline-based-education-research-understanding-and-improving-learning-in-undergraduate

This report synthesizes empirical research on undergraduate teaching and learning in the sciences, explores the extent to which undergraduate instruction reflects current evidence about learning and teaching, and identifies the intellectual and material resources required to further develop research in this areas. Knowledge of teaching and learning can mesh with deep knowledge of discipline-specific science content to provide detailed information on discipline-specific difficulties learners face in physics, biological sciences, geosciences, and chemistry.

Undergraduate Research Experiences for STEM Students: Successes, Challenges, and Opportunities (2017)
https://www.nap.edu/catalog/26024/undergraduate-and-graduate-stem-students-experiences-during-covid-19-proceedings

Undergraduate research experiences (UREs) have been proposed as tools to increase the active engagement of students and decrease traditional lecture-based teaching. This report provides a set of questions to be considered by those implementing UREs as one component of a learning system that engages students in STEM learning.

Barriers and Opportunities to 2- and 4-Year STEM Degrees: Systemic Change to Support Students Diverse Pathways (2016)
https://www.nap.edu/catalog/21739/barriers-and-opportunities-for-2-year-and-4-year-stem-degrees

This report describes changes in student demographics; how students, view, value, and utilize programs of higher education; and how institutions can adapt to support successful student outcomes. Students' decisions to enter, stay in, or leave STEM majors are impacted by the quality of instruction, grading policies, course sequences, undergraduate learning environments, student supports, co-curricular activities, students' general academic preparedness and competence in science, family background, and governmental and institutional policies. Many students do not take a traditional 4-year path to a STEM undergraduate degree and the report describes several other common pathways and also reviews what happens to those who do not complete the journey to a degree. The report raises the question of whether definitions and characteristics of what constitutes success in STEM needs to change.

Minority-Serving Institutions: America's Underutilized Resource for Strengthening the STEM Workforce (2019)
https://www.nap.edu/catalog/25257/minority-serving-institutions-americas-underutilized-resource-for-strengthening-the-stem

This report examines the nation's MSIs and identifies promising programs and effective strategies that have the highest potential return on investment for the nation by increasing the quantity and quality MSI STEM graduates. This study also provides critical information and perspective about the importance of MSIs to other stakeholders in the nation's system of higher education and the organizations that support them.

The Science of Effective Mentorship in STEMM (2019)
https://www.nap.edu/catalog/25568/the-science-of-effective-mentorship-in-stemm

Mentoring relationships provide developmental spaces in which students' skills in science, technology, engineering, mathematics, and medicine (STEMM) are honed and pathways into STEMM fields can be discovered. This report explores the importance of mentorship, the science of mentoring relationships, mentorship of underrepresented students in STEMM, mentorship structures and behaviors, and institutional cultures that support mentorship. This report and its complementary interactive, online guide present insights on effective programs and practices for institutions, departments, and individual faculty members.

Indicators for Monitoring Undergraduate STEM Education (2018)
https://www.nap.edu/catalog/24943/indicators-for-monitoring-undergraduate-stem-education

This report outlines a framework and a set of indicators that document the status and quality of undergraduate STEM education at the national level over multiple years to help policy makers and the public know whether reform initiatives are accomplishing their goals and leading to nationwide improvement in undergraduate STEM education.

Committee Member Biosketches

Margaret Honey (*Chair*) is president and CEO of the New York Hall of Science (NYSCI), which works to develop the next generation of creative science leaders through initiatives in teacher professional development, youth mentoring and employment, digital learning, learning sciences research and more. Under her leadership, NYSCI has developed its Design-Make-Play approach to learning, which helps learners experience their agency and creativity as creators and makers, master complex concepts and phenomena, and discover how they can put the tools and perspectives of the STEM disciplines to address questions and solve meaningful problems. Honey has helped to shape thinking about learning and technology with special attention to traditionally underserved audiences. She has directed numerous research projects including efforts to identify teaching practices and assessments for 21st century skills, new approaches to teaching computational science in high schools, collaborations with PBS, CPB, and some of the nation's largest public television stations, investigations of data-driven, decision-making tools and practices, and with colleagues at Bank Street College of Education, she created one of the first internet-based professional development programs in the country. From her early involvement in the award-winning and ground-breaking public television series "The Voyage of the Mimi" to her decade-long collaboration on the education reform team for the Union City (NJ) school district, Honey has led some of the country's most innovative and successful education efforts. She earned a B.A. in social theory at Hampshire College, Amherst, Massachusetts, and both her M.A. and Ph.D. in developmental psychology from Columbia University.

Rush D. Holt retired as chief executive officer of the American Association for the Advancement of Science and executive publisher of the *Science* family of journals where he led the world's largest multi-disciplinary scientific and engineering society. Before joining AAAS, Holt served for 16 years as a member of the U.S. House of Representatives, representing New Jersey's 12th Congressional District. In Congress, Holt served as a senior member of the Committee on Natural Resources and the Committee on Education. From 1987 to 1998, he was assistant director of the Princeton Plasma Physics Laboratory (PPPL), a Department of Energy national lab, which is one of the largest alternative energy research facilities in the country. At PPPL, Holt helped establish the lab's nationally recognized science education program. From 1980 to 1988, he was a member of the faculty of Swarthmore College, where he taught courses in physics and in public policy. Holt is a Phi Beta Kappa graduate of Carleton College in Northfield, Minnesota, and he holds M.A. and Ph.D. degrees in physics from New York University.

NANCY HOPKINS-EVANS is the senior director of State Partnerships at Instruction Partners where she uses her expertise and experience in science and education from kindergarten through graduate school to partner and support state education departments and regional service providers as they work to lead and guide their staff and district colleagues through operational, instructional and policy changes in the midst of a pandemic. As director of science and a former college chemistry professor, she understands and cares deeply about students having exceptional learning experiences in science that leverage their communities and cultures while building conceptual understanding as they figure out science ideas instead of learning about science through memorization of facts and theories. She has worked in large and small school systems developing and implementing curriculum, professional learning and assessment aligned to state standards, the common core state standards and the Next Generation Science Standards. She presents at conferences and leads professional learning experiences for teachers, principals, directors and superintendents focused on ensuring all students have access to high-quality standards and curriculum that supports effective teaching and learning. Her work in science education has been supported by grants from the Carnegie and Gates foundations to develop, test and refine a tool for observing and improving science instructional practice. She holds degrees in chemistry from Chestnut Hill College and Villanova University and earned a Ph.D. in biological chemistry from the University of Michigan.

TIFFANY NEILL is the deputy superintendent of Curriculum and Instruction for the Oklahoma State Department of Education. In addition, she is an active advisory board member for Carnegie's OpenSciEd Project and EdReports for Science and a member of the CALDER Policymakers Council. Neill also serves as co-principal investigator for Advancing Coherent and Equitable Systems of Science Education, a National Science Foundation-funded grant. Prior to her current role, she served as the executive director of Curriculum and Instruction for 3 years and as the director of Science and Engineering Education for 5 years at the Oklahoma State Department of Education. She began her career in education as a middle and high school teacher. Neill also served as president of the Council of State Science Supervisors and several other leaderships and service roles committed to fostering excellence in science education in Oklahoma and across the nation. She is currently a doctoral candidate at the University of Oklahoma, seeking a degree in instructional leadership and academic curriculum in science education.

STEPHEN PRUITT is president of the Southern Regional Education Board and former commissioner of education in Kentucky. In addition, he served as a senior vice president of science at Achieve, Inc. from 2010 to 2015. During this time, he led the development of the Next Generation Science Standards, Achieve's international benchmarking and analysis work, and other content-driven research and development as well as state technical assistance. Pruitt began his career as a high school chemistry teacher in Georgia, where he taught for 12 years. In 2003, he joined the Georgia Department of Education (GaDOE) as the program manager for science, served in that role for 4 years before becoming director of academic standards, in 2008 he became the associate superintendent of Assessment and Accountability and in April 2009 became chief of staff to state school superintendent, coordinating the work of the agency and a variety of projects such as Georgia's third-ranked Race to the Top application. He held a number of positions including chief of staff to the commissioner of education at Georgia Department of Education. Pruitt earned a bachelor's degree in chemistry from North Georgia College and State University, a master's in science education from the University of West Georgia, and a doctorate of philosophy in chemistry education from Auburn University.

FRANCISCO RODRIGUEZ is chancellor of the Los Angeles Community College District. Since 2014, Rodriguez has worked to chart a course that includes well-prepared and innovative faculty, state-of-the-art facilities and instructional equipment, superbly trained and professional support staff, and business and community engagement. During his tenure, Chancellor Rodriguez led the efforts to pass a $3.3 billion local facilities bond in 2016 and the hiring of close to six-hundred full-time faculty. A noted scholar/practitioner and education activist, he has 30+ years of experience as an educator, faculty member, and administrator within California public higher education. Rodriguez has dedicated his career to high-quality public education and championing diversity, equity and inclusion, and outreach to underserved communities. In particular, he has focused his career on educational policies that expand access to higher education, STEM education and financial aid, tireless advocacy for first-generation and undocumented students, student-veterans, and the leadership development of Latino and African American males. He frequently speaks on the topics of higher education, student access and success, governance and governing boards, workforce development, fundraising and philanthropy, and community. Rodriguez earned his bachelor's degree in Chicano studies and his master's degree in community development. He received his Ph.D. in education from Oregon State University.

SUSAN R. SINGER is vice president for academic affairs and provost at Rollins College, where she is responsible for administering the educational program, for making faculty appointments, for coordinating all academic activities of the College, for overseeing institutional and faculty research, for facilitating budgetary and institutional planning, and for maintaining the academic standards of the College. She served as the director of the Division of Undergraduate Education at the National Science Foundation, leading a team of 50 with a budget of more than $300 million annually to catalyze transformation in undergraduate learning and success across the nation. She helped lead the collaboration between 14 federal agencies to increase their collective impact on improving undergraduate science, technology, engineering, and mathematics education. She was a member of the Carleton College faculty from 1986-2016, where her experience included directing the Perlman Learning and Teaching Center and co-directing the Carleton Interdisciplinary Science and Math Initiative as well as research on the development and evolution of flowering in legumes. She was a co-author of the *Vision and Change in Undergraduate Biology* report. In addition, she chaired the NRC committee that produced *America's Lab Report* (2006) and the committee that wrote the report *Discipline-Based Education Research: Understanding and Improving Learning in Undergraduate Science and Engineering* (2012). Singer earned B.S., M.S., and Ph.D. degrees from Rensselaer Polytechnic Institute.

FELICIA C. SMITH is senior director of Global Delivery at the National Geographic Society, where she oversees domestic and global education strategy implementation and programming focused on transforming the classroom experience for millions of students and educators. She oversees a team of regional directors charged to enhance partnerships with various education entities to inspire the next generation of planetary stewards. Smith's career in education spans more than two decades where she has served in a variety of leadership roles in P-12, higher education, not-for-profit, and philanthropy. Her career has allowed her to experience leading systems understanding every vantage point of a young person's educational trajectory from preschool to adulthood. Prior to joining the National Geographic Society, she served as assistant superintendent of Teaching and Learning in the 27th largest urban district, Jefferson County Public Schools, Louisville, Kentucky; as a senior program officer at the Bill & Melinda Gates Foundation; associate commissioner for the Kentucky Department of Education; and teacher leader. She began her career as a classroom teacher in the elementary grades and has taught as a preservice lecturer at the University of Kentucky. She has been recognized as a Pahara-Aspen Education fellow and serves as a member on several national and local boards. Smith holds an Ed.D. in education leadership and administration from the University of Kentucky, a master's degree in elementary education with an emphasis on K-12 literacy development, and a bachelor's degree in elementary education from the University of Louisville.

WILLIAM F. TATE IV is the provost and executive vice president of academic affairs at the University of South Carolina (USC). He holds the USC Education Foundation Distinguished Professorship with appointments in Sociology and Family and Preventive Medicine (secondary appointment). Prior to joining the University of South Carolina faculty, he served as dean and vice provost for graduate education at Washington University in St. Louis, where he held the Edward Mallinckrodt Distinguished University Professorship in Arts & Sciences. Before serving at Washington University in St. Louis, he held the William and Betty Adams Chair at TCU and served on the faculty of the University of Wisconsin at Madison. He is a past president of the American Educational Research Association, where he was awarded fellow status. In addition, he was elected to the National Academy of Education. Tate earned his Ph.D. at the University of Maryland, College Park, where he was a Patricia Roberts Harris Fellow. He continued on to the University of Wisconsin at Madison as an Anna Julia Cooper Post-doctoral fellow in social policy. He completed a second postdoctoral training program in the Department of Psychiatry—Epidemiology and Prevention Group at the Washington University School of Medicine, where he earned a master's degree in psychiatric epidemiology.

CLAUDIO VARGAS is an educational consultant with Sci-Lingual Education. He provides Next Generation Science Standards (NGSS) professional learning to districts and schools to support multilingual learners with language and literacy development. Vargas presented at the National Academies Supporting ELs in STEM committee in 2017 and served in its panel in 2019, and frequently presents at statewide conferences and NGSS rollouts. Prior to this position, Vargas was the coordinator of K-12 science programs at the Oakland Unified School District (OUSD), where he led the district-wide implementation of the NGSS. Before joining OUSD, he served as the director of the Bay Area Science Project at UC Berkeley's Lawrence Hall of Science (LHS). Vargas designs K-8 professional development programs that focus on developing teachers' science content knowledge and expanding their instructional strategies, emphasizing methods that provide multilingual learners with access to the core curriculum and acceleration of language learning. He has led the implementation of these programs throughout California, Washington, Texas, and Central America. Before joining LHS, he worked for 9 years as a bilingual K-5 teacher and a science coach in the Oakland district, 11 years as a science researcher at the School of Pharmacy at the University of California, San Francisco, and 9 years at the Department of Bioengineering at the University of Minnesota.

BOARD ON SCIENCE EDUCATION

SUSAN SINGER (*Chair*), Vice President for Academic Affairs, Provost, Rollins College

SUE ALLEN, Maine Mathematics and Science Alliance

MEGAN BANG, Learning Sciences, Northwestern University

VICKI L. CHANDLER, Provost, Minerva Schools at Keck Graduate Institute

SUNITA V. COOKE, Superintendent and President, MiraCosta College

MAYA M. GARCIA, Science Content Specialist, Colorado Department of Education

RUSH HOLT, CEO Emeritus, American Association for the Advancement of Science

CATHY MANDUCA, Science Education Resource Center, Carleton College

JOHN MATHER, NASA Goddard Space Flight Center

TONYA MATTHEWS, CEO, International African American Museum

WILLIAM PENUEL, School of Education, University of Colorado Boulder

STEPHEN L. PRUITT, President, Southern Regional Education Board

K. RENAE PULLEN, K–6 Science Curriculum Instructional Specialist, Caddo Parish Schools, LA

K. ANN RENNINGER, Social Theory and Social Action, Swarthmore College

MARCY H. TOWNS, Bodner-Honig Professor of Chemistry, Purdue University

DARRYL N. WILLIAMS, Senior Vice President, Science and Education, The Franklin Institute

Staff

HEIDI SCHWEINGRUBER, *Director*

Acknowledgments

This report is grounded in decades of work on science education. The committee thanks all the researchers and practitioners who have improved our understanding of how people learn and how to provide better student experiences. We especially thank the hundreds individuals who provided feedback in response to our call for public input early in 2021 and the panelists who presented to the committee. We are deeply grateful to the committee members, reviewers, staff, and funders of previous National Academies of Sciences, Engineering, and Medicine reports related to science education, and especially the Carnegie Corporation of New York, which has funded this work, the *Framework for K-12 Science Education* (2012), and many other key efforts to improve science education. Thank you to Phil Gonring for serving as our writer. This Consensus Study Report was reviewed in draft form by individuals chosen for their diverse perspectives and technical expertise. We thank the following individuals for their review of this report: **Shafiq Chaudhary**, Math and Science Bureau, New Mexico Public Education Department; **Kelvin K. Droegemeier**, School of Meteorology, University of Oklahoma; **Sarah C. R. Elgin**, Department of Biology, Washington University in St. Louis; **Robert E. Floden**, College of Education, Michigan State University; **Maya Garcia**, Standards and Instructional Support, Colorado Department of Education; **Angela H. Quick**, Education Workforce Development, RTI International; **Ann Reid**, National Center for Science Education, Oakland, California; **Maria Chiara Simani**, California Science Project, and Physics Department, University of California, Riverside; **Nicole Smith**, Center on Education and the Workforce, Georgetown University; **Carl E. Wieman**, Department of Physics, Stanford University; and **Susan Gomez Zwiep**, BSCS Science Learning, Colorado Springs, Colorado.

Although the reviewers listed above provided many constructive comments and suggestions, they were not asked to endorse the conclusions or recommendations of this report nor did they see the final draft before its release. The review of this report was overseen by **Marshall (Mike) S. Smith, Palo Alto,** California, and **Edward Lazowska,** Department of Computer Sciences, University of Washington. They were responsible for making certain that an independent examination of this report was carried out in accordance with the standards of the National Academies and that all review comments were carefully considered. Responsibility for the content rests entirely with the authoring committee and the National Academies.

The National Academies of SCIENCES · ENGINEERING · MEDICINE

The National Academy of Sciences was established in 1863 by an Act of Congress, signed by President Lincoln, as a private, nongovernmental institution to advise the nation on issues related to science and technology. Members are elected by their peers for outstanding contributions to research. Dr. Marcia McNutt is president.

The National Academy of Engineering was established in 1964 under the charter of the National Academy of Sciences to bring the practices of engineering to advising the nation. Members are elected by their peers for extraordinary contributions to engineering. Dr. John L. Anderson is president.

The National Academy of Medicine (formerly the Institute of Medicine) was established in 1970 under the charter of the National Academy of Sciences to advise the nation on medical and health issues. Members are elected by their peers for distinguished contributions to medicine and health. Dr. Victor J. Dzau is president.

The three Academies work together as the **National Academies of Sciences, Engineering, and Medicine** to provide independent, objective analysis and advice to the nation and conduct other activities to solve complex problems and inform public policy decisions. The National Academies also encourage education and research, recognize outstanding contributions to knowledge, and increase public understanding in matters of science, engineering, and medicine.

Learn more about the National Academies of Sciences, Engineering, and Medicine at www.nationalacademies.org.

Consensus Study Reports published by the National Academies of Sciences, Engineering, and Medicine document the evidence-based consensus on the study's statement of task by an authoring committee of experts. Reports typically include findings, conclusions, and recommendations based on information gathered by the committee and the committee's deliberations. Each report has been subjected to a rigorous and independent peer-review process and it represents the position of the National Academies on the statement of task.

Proceedings published by the National Academies of Sciences, Engineering, and Medicine chronicle the presentations and discussions at a workshop, symposium, or other event convened by the National Academies. The statements and opinions contained in proceedings are those of the participants and are not endorsed by other participants, the planning committee, or the National Academies.

For information about other products and activities of the National Academies, please visit www.nationalacademies.org/about/whatwedo.

THE NATIONAL ACADEMIES PRESS 500 Fifth Street, NW Washington, DC 20001

This activity was supported by contracts between the National Academy of Sciences and Carnegie Corporation of New York (Award # G-21-58134) and the National Academy of Sciences W.K. Kellogg Foundation Fund. Any opinions, findings, conclusions, or recommendations expressed in this publication do not necessarily reflect the views of any organization or agency that provided support for the project.

International Standard Book Number-13: 978-0-309-47701-7

International Standard Book Number-10: 0-309-47701-8

Digital Object Identifier: https://doi.org/10.17226/26152

Library of Congress Control Number: 2021942155

Additional copies of this publication are available from the National Academies Press, 500 Fifth Street, NW, Keck 360, Washington, DC 20001; (800) 624-6242 or (202) 334-3313; http://www.nap.edu.

Copyright 2021 by the National Academy of Sciences. All rights reserved.

Printed in the United States of America

Suggested citation: National Academies of Sciences, Engineering, and Medicine. (2021). *Call to Action for Science Education: Building Opportunity for the Future.* Washington, DC: The National Academies Press. https://doi.org/10.17226/26152.

*America needs **better, more equitable science education.** We know America can deliver it.*